Lead Us Not Into Temptation

Other books by Don W. Basham

Face Up with a Miracle
Handbook on Holy Spirit Baptism
Spiritual Power: How to Get It and How to Live It
Deliver Us from Evil
True and False Prophets
The Miracle of Tongues
The Most Dangerous Game
Manual for Spiritual Warfare

Don Basham

Lead Us Not Into Temptation

Published by
√ chosen books

FLEMING H. REVELL COMPANY
OLD TAPPAN, NEW JERSEY

Note: The introduction and chapters four through ten contain material published in the author's previous book, *True and False Prophets*, Manna Books, Greensburgh, Pa., 1973.

Scripture quotations, unless otherwise indicated, are from the HOLY BIBLE: NEW INTERNATIONAL VERSION (North American Edition). Copyright © 1973, 1978, 1984, by the International Bible Society. Used by permission of Zondervan Bible Publishers.

Additional translations used are:
The Amplified New Testament, copyright © The Lockman Foundation 1954, 1958.
The Living Bible, copyright © 1971 by Tyndale House Publishers.
The King James Version.
New American Standard Bible, copyright © The Lockman Foundation 1960, 1962, 1963, 1968, 1971, 1972, 1973, 1975, 1977.

Library of Congress Cataloging in Publication Data

Basham, Don, 1926-
   Lead us not into temptation.

   "A Chosen book"—T.p. verso.
   1. Clergy—Professional ethics.   I. Title.
BV4011.5.B37   1986   174'.1   86-10245
ISBN 0-8007-9082-0

A Chosen Book
Copyright © 1986 by Don W. Basham

Chosen Books are published by
Fleming H. Revell Company
Old Tappan, New Jersey
Printed in the United States of America

To
Alice

Contents

Introduction

Balaam, the False Prophet

Many times the Bible warns us against false prophets, and a particular story in the Old Testament gives details concerning one such prophet's ministry. It is the story of Balaam, found in chapters 22 and 24 of the book of Numbers. This, briefly, is that account:

The Israelites have annihilated the Amorites and have pitched their tents in the plains of Moab. Balak, King of Moab, has heard the chilling news and gathers the princes of Moab and Midian together.

"We'll be swallowed up like an ox swallows the grass!" he laments. Then, in desperation, he sends some of his princes laden with money to recruit Balaam, a prophet of God, to come to Moab's aid.

"Come put a curse on these people," he has his princes tell Balaam, "for I know that those you bless are blessed and those you curse are cursed."

It is a rare opportunity for Balaam. The king has sent for his help and is ready to pay handsomely for it. Balaam eyes the bags of gold brought by the king's princes and says, "Spend the night here and I'll ask God if I may come with you."

Alone with God, Balaam explains how he's been asked by the King of Moab to curse Israel. To his dismay, God says, "You will not go with them and you will not curse Israel for Israel is blessed."

So Balaam returns to the king's men and says, "You may as well go home; God won't let me come with you."

The princes return to King Balak who immediately sends a larger delegation back to Balaam, upping the ante. He promises Balaam not only wealth, but anything else he wants if he will only come and curse Israel.

Balaam is driven by a lust for money and desperately wants the job. But remember, God's will has already been made known; he has been forbidden to go. So while he mouths the right words, "A palace full of silver and gold can't make me disobey God," Balaam's rebel heart seeks a way to accept the job. He tells the king's men to wait while he sees if God has changed his mind. Balaam clearly thinks God has made a mistake.

Rebellion always says, "I know better than God; my way is better than His." So God allows Balaam his rebellious way. "Since these men have come . . . go with them." With his rebel heart set on the gold and the new job, the next morning Balaam gets up, saddles his donkey, and says to Balak's princes, "Let's go!"

"But God was very angry when he went, and the angel of the Lord stood in the road to oppose him" (Numbers 22:22). Some will ask, "Why, if God let him go the second time, did God become angry?" Such a question reveals a lack of sensitivity to the ways of God. God's acquiescence must never be construed as God's commission. Anyone who moves only in God's acquiescence trespasses on God's grace and eventually tempts His wrath. Determined to show Balaam his folly, God sends an angel to oppose him.

Lust for wealth and position blinds Balaam's eyes to God's impending judgment, but the donkey Balaam is riding sees the angel and turns aside. Furious, Balaam beats the animal back into his own rebellious way. For a second and a third time the angel withstands Balaam and the donkey tries to halt: between walls where the donkey crushes Balaam's foot and in a narrow place where the donkey can only lie down.

Now Balaam's fury rises to murderous intensity. He's ready to kill the donkey, even after the donkey miraculously begins to speak. Finally, his eyes are opened to see the angel who says,

> "I have come here to oppose you because your path is a reckless one before me. The donkey saw me and turned away from me these three times. If she had not turned away, I would certainly have killed you by now, but I would have spared her."
>
> Numbers 22:32–33

Yet amazingly, Balaam's repentance is only partial!

> "I have sinned. I did not realize you were standing in the road to oppose me. Now *if* you are displeased, I will go back."
>
> Numbers 22:34, italics added

What staggering audacity is revealed in that word "if"! Balaam, knowing he is in rebellion, knowing his life hangs by a mere thread, says with feigned innocence, "*If* you are displeased. . . ."

But now it's too late. Balaam has chosen the rebel's course. He can neither turn back, nor can he curse Israel. The incidents that follow are profoundly ludicrous. Every time Balak says, "Try cursing Israel from this place," and Balaam opens his mouth, blessings for Israel pour forth. In fact, Balaam even ends up prophesying the coming of the Messiah:

> "I see him, but not now; I behold him, but not near;
> A star will come out of Jacob; a scepter will rise out of Israel. . . . A ruler will come out of Jacob. . . ."
>
> Numbers 24:17, 19

Balaam's inability to curse Israel eventually incurs King Barak's displeasure.

"I summoned you to curse my enemies, but you have blessed them these three times. Now leave at once and go home! I said I would reward you handsomely, but the Lord has kept you from being rewarded."

Numbers 24:10–11

In light of crucial matters we will be discussing later, it is essential to point out that Scripture clearly states that Balaam—even though he is a greedy and immoral rebel—is a prophet of God, "one who hears the words of God, who has knowledge from the Most High, who sees a vision from the Almighty" (Numbers 24:16). And while his greed, his immorality, and his rebellion do not prevent him from prophesying blessings for Israel, eventually they lead to his own death and terrible tragedy for the Israelites, who later give heed to his false counsel and join themselves to the worshipers of Baal. The Scriptures solemnly testify that 24,000 Israelites die because they follow Balaam's counsel (Numbers 25:1–9 and 31:15–16) and describe how Balaam himself is slain along with the kings of Midian (Numbers 31:8).

Centuries later, leaders in the New Testament church, when warning against false prophets and teachers, liken them to Balaam.

They have left the straight way and wandered off to follow the way of Balaam son of Beor, who loved the wages of wickedness. But he was rebuked for his wrongdoing by a donkey—a beast without speech—who spoke with a man's voice and restrained the prophet's madness.

2 Peter 2:15–16

Woe to them! They have taken the way of Cain; they have rushed for profit into Balaam's error; they have been destroyed in Korah's rebellion.

Jude 11

The book of Revelation describes the sin of Balaam even more clearly. To the church at Ephesus, Jesus said:

"Nevertheless, I have a few things against you: You have people there who hold to the teaching of Balaam, who taught Balak to entice the Israelites to sin by eating food sacrificed to idols and by committing sexual immorality."

Revelation 2:14

So what is the final portrait of Balaam? He was a false prophet; a man who spoke the true and exalted messages of God, even prophesying the coming of the Lord Jesus Christ, but whose life was governed by deceit, rebellion, lust, and greed.

Many of you may ask, "But how can a rebellious, greedy, and lustful man be an instrument for the ministry and message of God?" Well, Balaam was such a man. What's more, there are such men in ministry today, preying upon Christians and the church. I touched on this subject of unethical behavior in my book, *True and False Prophets*. Now, for the second time we are making a determined effort to expose and deal with that very problem.

Lead Us Not Into Temptation

1

The Invisible War

In the conclusion of his letter to the Ephesian church, Paul issues a strong challenge for us to engage in spiritual warfare:

> Finally, be strong in the Lord and in his mighty power. Put on the full armor of God so that you can take your stand against the devil's schemes. For our struggle is not against flesh and blood, but against the rulers, against the authorities, against the powers of this dark world and against the spiritual forces of evil in the heavenly realms.
>
> Ephesians 6:10–12

This book will portray a stark and dramatic picture of the warfare Paul describes. It will both document and address the tragic problems arising from an invisible war being waged against Christians and the church of Jesus Christ. While the evil effects of that war are plainly visible—immorality, deception, betrayal, wrecked and broken lives, slander and character assassination—the demonic forces creating such havoc are—at best—only dimly perceived and seldom opposed. Such ignorance not only assures

17

our failure to defeat our spiritual enemies, it often leads to our assisting them in their campaign to destroy us, the people of God. Jesus said this about such well-meaning but ignorant people:

> "They will put you out of the synagogue; in fact, a time is coming when anyone who kills you will think he is offering a service to God."
>
> John 16:2

Unfortunately, we often visualize warfare in an unrealistic way. We picture armies of infantry firing at one another across a "no-man's land," each side defending territory it already occupies. But the war we refer to is not being fought on a recognized battlefield with us on one side and "the enemy" on the other. Rather, Scripture reveals that in this invisible war, the Kingdom of God and the people of God are the battleground. Even though Jesus Christ did triumph over Satan on the Cross, the devil still stubbornly occupies territory he is no longer legally entitled to. So what has been legally *imputed* to us by Christ's death has not yet been fully *imparted* to us. One of the least understood realities of the Christian life today is this: *In this present age, the Kingdom of God is still partially occupied by the enemy!*

To no small degree we have misunderstood the nature of the Kingdom of God. The biblical account of the nation of Israel in its struggle to claim its inheritance in the Promised Land is a picture of the Christian's struggle to claim his inheritance in the Kingdom of God. God promised Israel the whole land of Canaan as its inheritance forever. But when it came time to occupy the land, the Israelites made a disturbing discovery; while Canaan was a land of unbelievable riches and abundance (see Numbers 13:27 and Deuteronomy 8:1–9), it was also occupied by giants, walled cities, and seven evil nations larger and stronger than Israel (see Numbers 13:31–33 and Deuteronomy 7:1–2).

Thus the Israelites learned the painful lesson that the battleground in the war to claim their inheritance was not somewhere outside the Promised Land, but was the Promised Land itself!

Like the spies sent by Moses to survey Canaan, we have glimpsed the wealth of the Kingdom of God; "the riches of his glorious inheritance in the saints" (Ephesians 1:18). But like Israel itself, we have often failed to drive the evil inhabitants out of our land.

In fact, the gospel is often presented as if our initial commitment to Jesus Christ were practically the end of the matter. The result has been that many converts—having been assured by some eager evangelist that once they accept Christ as Savior their problems are over—discover in dismay that the warfare has only begun! As my friend Bob Mumford has testified, "Before I was saved, all my Christian friends said, 'Bob, you need to accept Christ; that will solve all your problems.' So I took their advice and I accepted the Lord. Then I found I had a whole new set of problems!"

While acceptance of Jesus Christ as Savior settles our eternal destiny, victory over sin in this life remains to be won; and the warfare for the ultimate triumph of the Kingdom of God both within us and on earth goes on. So it is within—not outside—the boundaries of the Kingdom of God that the battle rages. And it is within—not outside—the life of the believer that the struggle for maturity and holiness is waged.

That great good and great evil can flourish in the same place at the same time and that men can be instruments of God one minute and tools of the devil the next, appear to be two of the least understood facts of the Christian life. The following personal experience illustrates the first fact.

For years I had heard stories of revivals where the glory of God supernaturally appeared as flames resting on top of the church building. I often wondered what it would be like to be in a service where such a manifestation took place. Then a few years ago at a church in a western state, I was the speaker at a seminar where some lives were dramatically changed by the power of God. On the final night I was sitting on the platform while the minister led the people into high realms of worship, waiting for my time to speak.

Far back in a corner of the large auditorium was a windowed

door that opened directly onto the church parking lot. Through the window I suddenly saw brightly blinking red lights, which indicated that some emergency vehicles had pulled up outside. Only later did I learn they were fire engines responding to a call from neighbors across the street who saw tall flames leaping into the sky above the church while the final service was in progress. With no way of knowing the "flames" were a supernatural sign of the presence of God resting on the meeting, they had called the fire department.

One might naturally expect such a spiritual manifestation to signify a high level of piety among the church's leaders and members. Sadly, that was not the case. At the same time I learned about the flames that drew the fire engines, I also learned the minister of the church had resigned after it was discovered that he was engaging in adultery with several female members of his congregation.

Great good and great evil can flourish in the same place at the same time.

In a parable in Matthew 13, Jesus describes the Kingdom of heaven as a field in which good and bad seed produce both wheat and weeds. But the owner (God the Father) decides to allow both wheat and weeds to grow and flourish alongside each other—*in the same field*—until the harvest. Then the wheat will be gathered and stored and the weeds will be burned.

Jesus identifies the Son of Man as the sower of the good seed, seed that "stands for the sons of the kingdom," and He describes the weeds as "the sons of the evil one" sown by the devil (verses 38–39). The separation of the wheat from the weeds does not take place until the end of the age.

> "As the weeds are pulled up and burned in the fire, so it will be at the end of the age. The Son of Man will send out his angels, and they *will weed out of his kingdom* everything that causes sin and all who do evil."
>
> Matthew 13:40–41, italics added

There is also scriptural support of the second misunderstood fact: that men can be instruments of God one minute and instruments of Satan the next. In Matthew 16 Peter declares Jesus to be the Christ, the Son of the living God, and immediately Jesus confirms his revelation: "Blessed are you, Simon son of Jonah, for this was not revealed to you by man, but by my Father in heaven" (verse 17).

But only five verses later, when Peter rebukes Jesus for speaking about His approaching death, Jesus says to him, "Out of my sight, Satan! You are a stumbling block to me; you do not have in mind the things of God, but the things of men" (verse 23).

How sobering to discover that Peter the Rock, Jesus' number one disciple, could serve as mouthpiece for God one minute, and mouthpiece for Satan the next. We will have much more to say about men being mouthpieces for Satan in chapters eleven through thirteen.

In 1 Corinthians 3 we find Paul addressing the same mixture of good and evil in the Kingdom of God. Having defined Jesus Christ as our foundation, he adds,

> If any man builds on this foundation using gold, silver, costly stones, wood, hay or straw, his work will be shown for what it is, because the Day will bring it to light. It will be revealed with fire, and the fire will test the quality of each man's work. If what he has built survives, he will receive his reward. If it is burned up, he will suffer loss; he himself will be saved, but only as one escaping through the flames.
>
> 1 Corinthians 3:12–15

Obviously, the "gold, silver, and costly stones" with which we build—and which emerge from the fires of testing intact—refer to gifts, ministries, and achievements that come from God's grace at work within us. Just as obviously, the "wood, hay or straw" with which Christians also try to build—and which are consumed in the fires of testing—are works of carnality and demonic deception, the fruit of the devil.

Finally, we see good and evil flourishing in the same person described in James' teaching about taming the tongue. Remember, he is writing to Christians:

> But no man can tame the tongue. It is a restless evil, full of deadly poison. With the tongue we praise our Lord and Father, and with it we curse men. . . . Out of the same mouth come praise and cursing. My brothers, this should not be.
>
> James 3:8–10

According to James, when a Christian speaks he can be either the mouthpiece for the Holy Spirit who blesses God, or the mouthpiece for Satan who curses both God and man. James then warns against a certain wisdom borne of bitter envy and selfish ambition that "is of the devil" and produces "disorder and every evil practice." (See James 3:14–16.) Then he describes a wisdom from heaven that is pure and peace-loving. (See verse 17.) Two kinds of speech—blessing and cursing—in the believer's mouth; two kinds of wisdom—one devilish, one heavenly—in the believer's mind. Good and evil flourishing in the same place. Let us say it again, *in this present age, the Kingdom of God is still partially occupied by the enemy.*

So in this book we are attempting to expose Satan's scheme for destroying the church of Jesus Christ. By tempting, provoking, deceiving, and seducing dedicated believers, he seeks to sear the Christian conscience until all traditional moral and spiritual values have been forsaken. Though eventually destined to fail, his presently successful strategy includes arousing unholy lusts that drive believers into immoral behavior that makes a mockery of marriage and covenantal love. It includes the use of prideful men who pervert the truth until divine grace becomes nothing more than amused toleration from an indulgent God who winks at sin. It includes the vicious and repeated verbal attacks on believers by other sincere believers who assume they have all the truth and refuse to accept personal accountability for the destructive effect of their words. Thus, an arrogant and unseen enemy continues to bully his way through the ranks of Christians, exploiting the church's reluctance to take a moral stand or raise an indignant voice in protest of his loathsome acts.

Sometimes God will show sensitive believers, through a dream or vision, the grave peril the church faces from evil forces lying in wait. Recently, a pastor friend sent me a letter in which he shared the chilling account of one such prophetic dream.

The Dream

I was standing in the middle of a small field surrounded by trees of several tropical varieties. I was not alone; there were twenty to twenty-five other men with me. I have no recollection of faces; I only knew we belonged to the same group.

Then, what appeared to be enemy soldiers emerged from under the trees, advancing toward us. We retreated only to discover soldiers converging on us from all sides. They herded us together into a tent about thirty feet long and twenty feet wide. It had a six-foot side wall, hanging loose and not quite touching the ground. We were forced into the middle of the tent and made to sit on the ground.

Suddenly, a new group of men entered the tent and somehow it was made known to me that they had come as our protectors. But instead of remaining alert and watchful, they lay down on their backs all around the inside of the tent and each of them thrust both his feet under the wall of the tent to the outside.

Only then did I become aware of the terrible activities taking place outside the tent. All the enemy soldiers disrobed and began to engage in a mass sexual orgy. Hundreds of bronzed bodies became involved in every kind of sexual perversion, right before my eyes. Stunned with horror, I watched as at regular intervals one of the naked soldiers would race up to grab the extended feet of one of our "protectors," jerk him out from under the tent and pass him on to one of the groups engaged in the acts of perversion.

When the last of the "protectors" had been abducted, the soldiers began snatching men from the group sitting with me, one by one. It wasn't long until I was the only one left. I stood fearfully at one end of the tent, knowing that the soldiers would soon come for me. Yet somehow—in the midst of that terrifying nightmare, shaking with fear over what I knew might happen to me—I realized I could pray for protection. Just before the soldiers came for me I pled with God for grace enough not to respond to anything they might do to me. I had no sooner prayed when several naked soldiers seized me and dragged me out of the tent. Just as one of the men leaned down to molest me, I was able to break out of the dream, struggle up out of bed, and grope my way into the living room and turn on the light.

After the Dream

While the light afforded a measure of relief, if I closed my eyes I could feel the awful nightmare beginning again. I felt as if my very sanity were being threatened. I paced back and forth in my living room, crying out to God for help. It was only after repeatedly singing, "Bless the Lord, O my soul: and all that is within me bless His holy name," that relief came. It took ninety minutes of singing, plus desperate, agonizing prayer before the awful vision finally receded and I regained a perspective that was sane and rational. As I sat exhausted on the sofa, I realized I had experienced something far more significant than just a simple nightmare. I had been given a sober spiritual warning.

An Evaluation

When a measure of peace finally returned and I regained most of my composure, the spiritual significance of what I had just experienced began to break in on me. I felt God was showing me that the "protectors" in my dream were pastors and ministers who were insensitive and indifferent in regard to guarding their flocks, and whose desire to walk in both the spiritual and carnal worlds at the same time (as evidenced by their feet being extended outside the tent) would prove disastrous for many of them. I felt God was showing me that in the days ahead, every pastor or shepherd called to protect the people of God will be increasingly subjected to demonic temptations of all kinds, particularly sexual temptation.

I saw that as the level of spiritual warfare in the church continued to intensify, increasing numbers of pastors and spiritual leaders would be seduced by demonic forces, and would abandon the congregations they were called to pastor and protect, leaving their people open to Satanic attack as well. For days after that strange, terrifying experience I found myself earnestly praying for God to help me find a way to warn our nation's pastors and spiritual leaders of the peril they face.

That minister's dream is already a nightmare of reality for many believers. Christian readers of the July 1985 *Ladies' Home Journal* were undoubtedly shocked by an anonymous article entitled "My Minister Kept Making Passes." The sordid account described the plight of a church secretary whose boss couldn't keep his hands off her. A married woman with a semi-invalid husband, she needed her job desperately and for several months endured the sexual harassment of the minister, while managing to avoid outright immorality. The article detailed her agonizing struggle, not only to avoid being seduced by the minister but to find responsible, mature Christians to help her in her dilemma. After learning that two other women in the church had been similarly accosted, she sought help from the minister's superiors, only to be told that unless she and the other women publicly confronted the minister, nothing could be done. Even then, they were told, there was no assurance he would be removed from ministry. Eventually, the minister—piously protesting that his "affectionate gestures" had been misunderstood—was transferred, and the offended women suffered painful and unjust condemnation by church members who refused to believe their stories and sided with the minister. The author's closing observations are significant:

> Throughout this entire ordeal, I feel that what hurt me the most was the automatic assumption that because the charges were made against a minister, they must be lies. People simply do not want to believe a minister could do something immoral. At church I pray for Reverend Smithson and hope he will come to acknowledge the immorality of his behavior and get help. I also pray for the unsuspecting women he will be working with. Finally, I pray hardest for my fellow churchgoers. I pray that they will recognize that spiritual leaders are human. . . .

While the secretary's confession undoubtedly shocked many readers of *Ladies' Home Journal*, it was no surprise to many of us in ministry. In fact, I felt she should be grateful to have escaped actual sexual seduction since many women caught in her situation do not.

Some time ago, during meetings in a church in a large city, I was approached for counseling by a woman who tearfully confessed to an extramarital affair with a prominent local clergyman. She refused to divulge his name. The next day, I spoke with another young woman who also confessed to a lengthy adulterous affair, apparently with the same minister. Neither woman would name the man because they said he was a highly admired spiritual leader in the city, and besides, they were not sure anyone would believe them. I flew home wondering darkly how many more women the lustful minister had seduced.

Then a few weeks later, during a Bible teaching mission in a certain eastern city, a lovely young woman made an appointment to see me.

"Reverend Basham," she said as we sat in the pastor's study, "I have a problem so unusual I hardly know how to tell you about it. [It wasn't nearly as unusual as she thought.] A few weeks ago, our church sponsored an evangelist whose preaching was just wonderful. Many people were saved and blessed. It was a wonderful week of ministry. . . ." She paused and her eyes filled with tears. "But it wasn't a wonderful week for me. I know the minister was a servant of God since God used his ministry in such a wonderful way, only. . . ." She paused again.

"The very first night he began looking at me in a way that made me uncomfortable. And after the service he squeezed my hand and said the Lord had shown him I was a very special person. I was flattered but also embarrassed because his manner was so familiar.

"The next night after the service," the young woman continued, "he sought me out again. He took both my hands in his and told me the Lord had shown him he could be a father to me. Only, Reverend Basham, he wasn't looking at me like a father, but in a way that made me feel undressed.

"The third night he said the Lord had shown him he could be a 'spiritual husband' to me. Worst of all, at two o'clock in the morning, my telephone rang. It was the evangelist calling me from his motel room. He begged me to come and join him. He claimed God was showing him many wonderful things about me and that it was essential for him to share them with me immediately and not to tell anyone where I was going.

"I was so upset, all I could do was slam down the receiver. I didn't have the nerve to attend any more of his services, because I knew he wanted to have an affair with me. No man who invites a woman to his motel room at two o'clock in the morning has right motives, I don't care how great a preacher he is. But Reverend Basham, how could he ask me to do such a thing? I just don't understand."

The young woman was right; she didn't understand, just as the secretary who wrote the magazine article didn't understand, and just as thousands of other Christians don't understand. That young woman wasn't aware of even a fraction of that immoral minister's reputation. I have received many letters from responsible, heartsick Christians in many parts of the country about him, Christian fathers and husbands whose daughters and wives had been seduced by him. Yet he is still in ministry, still winning people to Christ with unbelievable effectiveness.

Of course, the moral problems of ministers include more than sexual immorality. Some years ago, a controversial evangelist known for his dramatic ministry of healing was found dead in a hotel room with thousands of dollars in his pockets. After an autopsy showed he had died of acute alcoholism, newspapers across the country had a field day with articles exposing his weakness for alcohol, his questionable handling of finances, and questioning the validity of his controversial ministry.

Many believers were deeply puzzled and hurt about the reports since authenticated miracles of healing followed his ministry up until the time of his death. A personal friend of mine related how he saw this evangelist appear backstage at his own meeting so drunk he could scarcely stand. Yet when the time to preach arrived, he suddenly sobered up, strode on stage and ministered with powerful results. Immediately after the service he resumed his drinking.

When, without mentioning his name, I commented on this minister's tragic plight in a magazine article, I received some scathing letters from loyal disciples who said that those who claimed the evangelist had a drinking problem were enemies out to destroy his ministry. They insisted that when he seemed to stagger on stage, it was just a sign of the heavy spiritual anointing that was upon him. One letter that bitterly castigated me claimed the doctor who performed the autopsy on the evangelist's body was an avowed Communist, out to destroy the reputation of a man of God. Several months later, I received a second letter asking my forgiveness. In the interval the writer had learned the sad truth that the evangelist he so greatly admired had indeed become an alcoholic before he died. His letter ended with a familiar question. "I loved the man and believed in his ministry. How could he minister with such power when his personal life was so fouled up?" How indeed!

Just a few weeks ago I had a personal conversation with a minister of one of the largest churches in the United States who serves on a regional morals and ethics committee of his denomination. He revealed to me how, at that very time, his committee was dealing with eighteen specific cases of confessed sexual immorality involving ministers in their region of the country alone.

How can a minister whose personal life is a moral shambles, who is guilty of repeated dishonesty and immorality, continue to exercise an effective ministry attested to by conversions and signs and wonders? I know of no more pressing challenge in the church today than for Christians to be able to answer that question, and to become wisely alert and prepared to deal with the problem of false ministers. For this is how we must classify the men we have been describing. They are *false* ministers of Christ.

In the chapters that follow we will be discussing at length the problem of moral laxity in the church and its ministry. And the problems are not limited to just sexual immorality or financial dishonesty, as loathsome as those sins are. We will also examine other, more subtle and more destructive forms of immorality: the "respectable" sins of spiritual rape and seduction—slander, libel, false accusation, and character assassination—spawned by Christians' hatred for and jealousy of one another. It is no accident that Paul lists hatred, jealousy, and selfish ambition alongside sexual immorality, impurity, and debauchery as works of the flesh that can lead to exclusion from the Kingdom of Heaven (see Galatians 5:19–21). And it is no mere coincidence that John the Revelator leaves outside the gates of the City of God not only magicians, murderers, and sex offenders, but those who love and practice falsehood as well (see Revelation 22:15).

But in our determination to face our problems we dare not lose sight of the fact that the real enemy is not people—weak and even wicked as some of them are. Our real enemy is the prince of darkness who, with all his demonic hosts, has set himself in unrelenting opposition to the redemptive purposes of God in the earth and to all that is pure and holy.

So, in spite of the nightmarish revelation we shared, and in spite of all the other unpleasant facts we will examine in the pages ahead, we need to keep the right perspective and remember that our struggle is not against flesh and blood and that the ultimate triumph of the Kingdom of God has already been assured. So as you read, take comfort in the knowledge that the Lord brings sordidness to light not to hinder but to help, not to condemn but to cleanse, so that when He returns, it will be for a bride "without stain or wrinkle or any other blemish" (Ephesians 5:27).

2

True and False Prophets

It was some years ago that I first wrote a book about immorality and unethical behavior among Christians. I wrote with some haste in the hope that my brief, introductory survey of the subject would encourage other Christian writers and teachers to examine the problem in greater depth. But today, a decade later, that hope remains largely unfulfilled; I know of no other book specifically addressing the subject and my first book is long out of print. Yet the crisis of immoral and unethical behavior among believers—including Christians in leadership—seems to have grown steadily worse.

I wrestled with the problem for several years before deciding to write about it. As an author and Bible teacher involved in the charismatic renewal since 1963, I had seen thousands of Christians experience new life and power in the Holy Spirit. But it didn't take long for me to discover that new blessings did not put an end to old problems. In the counseling and correspondence that accompany any public teaching ministry, I found myself listening to an endless stream of confessions by troubled believers whose personal problems seemed to deny the faith they professed.

Many were trapped in dishonest or immoral relationships with other Christians, including Christian ministers.

On occasion I even found myself sharing leadership in conferences with men who had powerful public ministries, but whose private lives were a blatant contradiction of their public teaching. But because their immoral behavior was not generally known—or at least not publicly admitted—they often took advantage of the very people receiving their ministry.

I remember a seminar in a western state where I spoke on spiritual warfare. Later in the prayer room, under the ministry of several mature leaders, many people were set free from demonic torment. But there was one troubled young divorcee we could not help; she became hysterical and rushed out of the prayer room, sobbing. Afterward, one of the conference speakers who had declined to help us in the ministry was waiting outside the door. He was furious. The young woman who had rushed from the room was seated near him, still crying.

"What were you men trying to do to this girl, Basham?" he shouted. "Every time people get near you, they start imagining they have demons! That deliverance ministry of yours causes nothing but trouble."

Before I could answer, he grabbed the girl by the hand and hauled her away. A short time later it became public knowledge that the angry minister was, in fact, engaged in an adulterous relationship with the young woman, an affair that led to the breakup of his own marriage. No wonder she couldn't receive deliverance; no wonder he became so angry.

From such experiences I came to realize that spiritual anointing and power in a Christian's life are no guarantee of moral or spiritual integrity. "Watch out for false prophets," Jesus warned. "By their fruit [not their gifts!] you will recognize them" (Matthew 7:15–16). In fact, the naive and unscriptural belief that effective ministry is proof of righteous character is one of the most dangerous of all fallacies. It has allowed Satan to create havoc in the Body of Christ. Exposing that fallacy and correcting the religious naiveté that sustains it was to become a major goal of my first book on this subject.

Yet making the final decision to write the book proved difficult. Regardless of what seemed to be a genuine prompting from the Holy Spirit, something inside me recoiled at the thought of writing on such a painful subject. Neither was I anxious to stir up more trouble—since the deliverance ministry in which I was involved was providing more than a little controversy already. Besides, who was I to talk about other people's problems, anyway? Wouldn't I be accused of sitting in judgment? Wouldn't it appear that I considered myself better than those who had fallen into Satan's snare? While a loving wife and happy marriage gave me a security that some men in ministry did not have, I knew I was no more deserving than others who had fallen, only more fortunate. In my case, opportunity for misconduct seemed providentially to coincide with times when I felt spiritually secure.

I recall the last night of a meeting in a northern city where— during prayer at the church altar—a number of people were visibly touched by the power of God. One of them, a young woman with a stunning figure, warmly embraced me in a manner that communicated more than spiritual gratitude. Embarrassed, I peeled her arms from around my neck, said something about giving God the glory, and turned to pray with someone else.

At seven A.M. the next morning at my motel, I was already dressed and packed when there was a knock on my door. When I opened it, there stood the same sexy young lady, dressed even more provocatively. She breathed something about needing counseling and started past me into the room. Grabbing her firmly by the arm, I said, "We can talk while I have breakfast." Safely seated in the coffee shop, I listened to her tearful recitation about an unhappy marriage to a wealthy older man who seemed largely oblivious to his wife's physical charms. "I'm so hungry for love and affection, I'm ready to have an affair!" she said frankly.

Trying not to looked shocked, I expressed sympathy for her plight, suggested that she and her husband find an understanding marriage counselor as soon as possible, and reminded her I had a plane to catch. Then I raced to my room for my luggage, caught the airport limousine, and forty-five minutes later was safely aboard the plane, heading home to my wife and children.

But even as I thanked God for protecting me that day, sober

memories of other days came to mind: low, despairing days of doubting God, days that left me struggling against unholy, mind-searing thoughts that never found expression in outward conduct. Had opportunity for sin ever appeared at such a time, avoiding Satan's snare would have proved far more difficult.

But for all my reservations and unanswered questions, the problem of immorality and unrighteous behavior in the Body of Christ seemed so great, and the prompting of the Holy Spirit seemed so insistent, I felt I had to say something.

My first attempt took place in a Bible seminar in West Palm Beach, Florida. I remember the occasion vividly because of the audience's unexpected reaction to my teaching. In my message that evening I began by sharing some thoughts on the differences between the *gifts* of the Holy Spirit, which are manifestations of God's supernatural power, and the *fruit* of the Spirit, which reflects righteous character. I stressed the need for both. Then I cited some scriptural examples of leaders who fell into immorality. I also shared some carefully disguised illustrations of contemporary influential Christians whose lives had been wrecked by dishonesty or immorality. I ended the message with a fervent plea for personal righteousness and holiness. While I felt the Holy Spirit's approval as I spoke, public response was not what I expected.

The audiences I normally faced were conditioned to hearing messages on spiritual renewal, faith, healing, and deliverance. They were so used to hearing testimonies of answered prayer, and hearing how the power of God could be more fully released in their own lives, they were shocked and stunned by my blunt warnings about dishonesty and immorality. And their reactions quickly showed it.

I was accustomed to people coming forward after a message to ask questions, to express appreciation, or to seek ministry. But this time the group was much smaller than usual and mostly hostile. Some frankly said they didn't believe me. Others asked sharp, critical questions I could not answer, making me aware that I needed to make a more thorough scriptural study of the whole subject. One man—a minister—said he believed it was highly inappropriate to speak publicly about such sensitive matters. The barrage of criticism tempted me to drop the whole subject permanently.

Fortunately, among the crowd of critics were a few people who seemed grateful, saying things like, "I've been waiting for years for someone to tell it like it is." I was most affected by the confession of a woman who drew me aside to speak in private. She had become sexually involved with a prominent Bible teacher and had suffered months of deep distress and guilt before finding forgiveness and restoration with God.

"I was weak and foolish in allowing myself to be seduced," she confided, "and I know God has forgiven me. But what distresses me most is the attitude of the minister who took advantage of me. He became furious when I broke off the affair, but publicly he still preaches and teaches as if nothing happened. Shouldn't something be done to correct or discipline him?" Her testimony and her plaintive question helped keep my resolve alive.

Final encouragement to write the book came from a conversation with Len LeSourd and his wife, the late Catherine Marshall. The LeSourds were members of the editorial board of Chosen Books which, only a few months earlier, had published my book, *Deliver Us from Evil.* One evening when my wife, Alice, and I were having dinner with them the conversation turned to the subject of my next book. When Catherine heard I was considering writing on morals and ministry but was feeling reluctant to tackle such a sensitive subject, she shared something that occurred during the writing of her best-selling novel, *Christy.*

In Catherine's novel, Miss Alice Henderson, a Quaker missionary, confesses to a shocked and protesting Christy how—as a sixteen-year-old girl—she had been seduced by a Quaker evangelist. In the book, her tragic confession covers an entire chapter. I have extracted only a few paragraphs.

When I was just turned thirteen, an itinerant preacher, a Quaker from England, first visited us. . . . This man came back the next year and the next. . . . When my parents were not around he began to tell me of a new and delightful discovery . . . a divine electricity which could flow . . . through laying hands on the body of another. He opened the Bible to passage after passage to show me how Jesus had laid His hands on people. . . .

I believed all this because I trusted the man. . . . Also I believe that he had a number of such situations underway in different stages so that he was content to bide his time for me.

When I was fifteen there was a certain amount of experimentation, what he called "laying on of hands" . . . but because I was so ignorant of sex, I interpreted the thrill in exactly the high-flown spiritual way the man meant for me to interpret it. So the groundwork was all laid and eagerly I looked forward to the man's visit that spring when I was sixteen. . . .

My parents trusted him implicitly. Word had not yet reached Pennsylvania that the man's teaching and ministry had been sharply discredited in England.

One afternoon when my parents were gone . . . he told me there was a way to have wave upon wave of spiritual blessing which one felt as a physical thrill through one's body. But he would have to show me. Was I game? . . . I should remove some of my clothes in order to feel the thrill best. . . .

Mercifully, I'll draw the curtain there . . . except to say that when he was finished, I was weeping violently, crumpled up at his feet, no longer a virgin. . . . By the next month I guessed I was "with child". . . .

Father was a gentle man. . . . I had not known he was capable of such anger. He spent great sums of money with secret agents in the British Isles trying to track down the man. But it was no use.[1]

"When my editor first read that part of my manuscript he was troubled," Catherine Marshall recalled. "He said, 'Catherine, your Christian readers will be scandalized by such a sordid story. I don't think it belongs in your book.' "

But Catherine refused to delete it. "I often feel the Holy Spirit is helping me when I write," she continued. "And I told my editor that day I had never been more certain of the Holy Spirit's leading than when I wrote that shocking story, because it was based

[1] *Christy*, Catherine Marshall, McGraw-Hill Pub., N.Y., N.Y., 1967.

on a true experience I knew about. Indeed, I felt as if it were written by the hand of the Holy Spirit Himself. I insisted that it remain in the manuscript!"

Then she went on to tell how, when the bookstore association of a large denomination read *Christy* in its advanced proof stage they vowed not to order any copies of the book unless that section was deleted. Again Catherine refused. When the book was published, the bookstore association ordered copies anyway.

Then, Catherine Marshall looked me squarely in the eye. "Don, you have chosen a subject that—unpleasant as it sounds—is of vital importance. Don't let anything or anyone stop you from writing that book."

So, gathering my resolve, I began compiling material for the book and quickly made three discoveries. First, my more thorough study of Scripture revealed an astonishing amount of teaching on the subject of morals and ministry. Secondly, as I studied relevant Scripture passages I became alarmed at how ignorant most Christians—including myself—are about how the grace of God works. Most of us have inaccurate, unscriptural, preconceived ideas about what God ought to do and not do, and about whom He should and should not choose for His work. Those unscriptural ideas have greatly contributed to our inability to confront or even acknowledge immoral behavior in the midst of vital Christian activity.

Thirdly, from personal correspondence and notes from numerous counseling sessions, I saw the need to divide those involved in immoral and dishonest situations into two groups: the one group I labeled weak, the other group I labeled wicked. One group was victims; the other group was victimizers.

I felt quick compassion for those Christians in the first group who fell into sin accidentally, or who were trapped by Satan unexpectedly. But the second group included those who were not simply unfortunate victims, guilty of some momentary moral lapse, but those who had become habitual offenders, cunning and deceptive, unable or unwilling to control their evil desires. They had become the "false prophets," the "ravenous wolves" Jesus spoke of in Matthew 7:15, using their God-given gifts with disarming effectiveness, only to later take scandalous advantage of some of the very people their ministries had helped. It was these false ministers I sought to warn people about, with the fervent hope that the Body of Christ might not only become alert to the danger but also willing to work together for the removal of such people from the ministry.

But my task was made even more difficult by the painful realization that many of these same "false prophets" were men who originally had a heart after God and who, for all their tragic problems, still longed to minister His grace. Driven by their own uncontrollable desires, but left free to continue their double lives by the very naiveté of Christians who found it inconceivable that grace and sin could both operate so powerfully in the same person, they seemed doomed to a kind of "Dr. Jekyll/Mr. Hyde" destiny, creating more wreckage in the Kingdom of God than all the good their God-anointed ministries were able to produce. Was there no hope for any of them, or might some be saved? I wasn't sure.

I decided to call my book *True and False Prophets*.

3

Reactions to a Controversial Message

When *True and False Prophets* reached the public, reaction was immediate. Since the subject had been controversial when I spoke about it, I should have known the book would prove controversial as well. But I was not prepared for the intensity of feeling it provoked in its readers. While other books I have written proved to have a wider readership, none created a more divided readership. As letters from readers began to arrive I found myself alternately praised and criticized, blessed and damned. It seemed that no one was neutral on the subject. Either the book was very good or very bad; and I was either inspired by God or deceived by the devil, depending on which group of letters I examined.

One minister, deeply offended by an excerpt from the book that appeared in *New Wine Magazine*, didn't hesitate to let the editors know how he felt:

Dear New Wine Editor:
    Please remove my name from your mailing list immediately. I am very careful as to the type of literature entering my home. Such articles as "Let's Face It: We Have This Problem" by some

fellow named Basham is not worth printing or reading. His implication that God is so bad off for vessels to use that He must resort to immoral, sinful, and uncleansed people is so absurd that it deserves no rebuttle or debate. Please destroy the next issue to be sent to me.

Similar letters arrived in a steady stream at my home. Some who disagreed with the book not only rejected what I wrote, they labeled me variously as insane, deceived, Satanic, a sex pervert, or a Communist. One irate female reader sent me a package by registered mail. It contained a copy of *True and False Prophets* with a huge black "X" marked through every page in the book! There was also a personal letter filled with scathing denunciation that ended with the comment, "I'm praying that God will forgive you for writing such a horrible book!" I concluded that something in the book struck a sensitive nerve.

Fortunately, the letters of appreciation substantially outnumbered the letters of criticism. Nevertheless, to have one-fourth of your readers challenge the message you've labored so diligently to communicate is a painful experience. And even the appreciative letters were often painful to read because of the tragic testimonies they contained.

The decision to share the following excerpts from some of those letters was a difficult one. To expose to public view—even in a way that protects privacy—the struggles and heartaches of certain Christians, certain pastors, and certain churches who have become victims of unscrupulous ministers is not a pleasant task. But I do it with the hope that the indignation that is likely to follow reading such material can be tempered with pity and compassion and eventually shaped into some form of remedial action. God knows something needs to be done.

Here are excerpts of an eight-page letter from a 27-year-old housewife in an eastern city:

Dear Mr. Basham,
    It is 1:00 A.M. I have just finished reading *True and False Prophets*. I am not an avid reader, but I could not put your book down. As I read, the Holy Spirit spoke to my heart in ways too

numerous to count. Every page held new truths for me—answers to long-time questions and confirmations I have sought for years. How I praise God. . . .

I had been many places seeking counsel for my troubled marriage and finally began seeing the minister of a church just down the street. I even joined the church. After a few counseling sessions I began to feel personally attracted to him.

He told me that often happened between Christians and their pastors, that it was all right with him, and that he would "fill in for my husband." Three days later we began an affair. . . . I was constantly riddled with guilt and fear, but he continued to preach and win souls and profess he didn't feel guilty. . . . When I tried to protest the sexual part of our relationship he said, "When you truly care for someone you must express it fully."

Then, all at once he changed and began to say we should be more Christian and refrain from letting our emotions rule us. I soon discovered he had become involved with another woman in the church. When I confronted him, he threatened to sue me if I said anything to anyone. I was terrified! I stopped seeing him and left the church. Later, the other woman confessed to her husband who told church authorities and the man was put out of the ministry.

I thank God He has forgiven me. I pray every minister of the Gospel will read and believe what you have written.

Other letters contained similar confessions:

"I never understood how Christians could do such things until I read your book. . . ."

"Thank God we received your book just in time. We confronted our minister with it and he has resigned. . . ."

"I could scarcely believe it when a well-known Bible teacher attempted to seduce my wife. Then I read *True and False Prophets*. . . ."

"I lived with guilt for years until I read your book. I thought I must have done something to provoke a certain minister's unholy lust for me. Now I understand he had fallen into Satan's snare."

"Your book helped me understand what happened to me. I loaned my minister $6,000 from my late husband's estate. He promised to pay it back in three years but left the church after six months. That was four years ago and I've never heard from him. . . ."

There were also copies of letters written on official church stationery withdrawing endorsement from certain ministries. Any sensitive person must wince at the unspoken grief and heartache that lie just beneath the surface of these guarded, carefully worded statements. One from Florida said:

"We regret to inform you that we have found the above-named person guilty of repeated immorality. Therefore, we have withdrawn our endorsement of his ministry and consider ourselves no longer affiliated with him. Your prayers are urgently needed for this minister. . . ."

Also included was a copy of the letter of dismissal written to the minister himself:

Dear Brother _____,
> We deeply regret to inform you that your ordination with _____ Church is no longer in effect, as of this date.
> On the basis of proven testimony given us concerning your immoral behavior, this board has no other alternative. We pray diligently that you will repent and that you may eventually be restored to the ministry. We are available for counsel if you desire. . . .

Then, from a church in a northern state came this sad epistle:

To Whom It May Concern:
> According to the guidelines given to us in holy Scriptures we, the elders of this assembly, declare Rev. _____ to be a false teacher and grossly immoral.
> Over a year ago we confronted Rev. _____ about [his conduct] and he flatly declared his innocence. We felt at the time we had to accept his denial. At this meeting and many times afterward we warned him about visiting women alone. He ignored our warning. . . .

Since that meeting he has approached six women in our own congregation, in hopes of seducing them. We have two tape recordings of his lurid conversations.

On this evidence we have proceeded to revoke his license to preach. [We feel] we have obeyed the guidelines found in the 18th chapter of Matthew in dealing with this situation. At first he agreed to close out his ministry, but later changed his mind. Therefore, this letter had to be composed as a warning to the flock.

This letter will also be circulated to other churches.

The document was signed by the six elders of the church and by the six women the minister had either seduced or attempted to seduce. An accompanying letter to me stated that not only had the minister refused to repent, he had split the church taking half the congregation with him, and was holding services in another building across town.

The difficulty in trying to remove an immoral minister out of ministry and keep him out until his life shows true fruit of repentance is made even worse by other unwise leaders who are sometimes much too quick to offer absolution and much too eager to proclaim the problem solved. In light of the sworn statements in the official document just quoted, I was shocked a few days later to receive a copy of another "To Whom It May Concern" letter about the same minister. The second letter was mailed from the office of a nationally known evangelist who, after superficial and hasty counseling with the immoral minister, rather than insisting he remove himself from ministry for a period of discipline and correction, pronounced him fit for ministry. His letter concluded with this statement:

With a full awareness of the severity of the charges and of the seriousness of my commitment, I commend Rev. _____ as being worthy of your consideration in the capacity of a minister of the Gospel of our Lord Jesus Christ.

Such sentimental and unrealistic pronouncements simply serve to compound the problem. Moreover, effective ministry to those who have been victimized by an immoral minister and efforts to restore integrity to their lives are made even more difficult by the knowledge that some of the "victims" are not totally blameless themselves.

About a year after receiving the first "To Whom It May Concern" document, I ministered at a conference in a city not far from the troubled church that issued it. I remember well the frustration I felt following a counseling session with a young couple from that church who came and sought me out. With her forlorn young husband at her side, the wife vividly described her "ordeal" as one of the women in the church who had been seduced. She told how the minister came to her home one morning for an early pastoral call, and "before I knew what was happening he had me in bed with him." She professed shock and surprise but added, "I just knew no one would believe me if I told them our very own preacher had seduced me right in my own home."

Unfortunately, she still couldn't decide whether or not to say anything after several additional mornings in bed with him. In fact, far from being in tears over her misfortune, she seemed to enjoy trying to shock me with the details of a sexual encounter she clearly had not found all that tragic.

During the same conference I also met the tearful ex-wife of a fallen minister. It seems that only a few weeks after the attempt by the nationally known evangelist to pronounce him restored, he had become sexually involved with yet another young woman in his church. This time, he divorced his wife to marry his latest conquest. Sympathetic Christian friends were providing care for the forsaken first wife and her three children.

Fortunately, some stories had happier endings. At a seminar in an eastern state a tall young minister with sad eyes sought me out. "I read your book on false prophets," he said, "and I'm afraid I qualify as one. Can you help me?"

Then he explained how, in addition to pastoring a small church, he also served on the faculty of a conservative Bible college where he met and fell in love with a girl student. Since the college forbade dating between faculty and students, he and his girlfriend had resorted to meeting secretly off campus. His girlfriend suspected she was pregnant. Trapped between his ministry and his love for the girl he was filled with guilt.

"Do you think God can forgive me for the mess I've made of things?" he asked.

Recognizing his problem as one of weakness and not wickedness, I suggested a possible solution. "I don't think you really qualify as a false prophet," I said. "Why don't you resign from the church and college, ask God for forgiveness, marry the girl you love, and begin a fresh life and ministry in some other part of the country?"

Several months later I received a letter from him. He and his bride were safely settled in a city in another state where he found work as a television repairman. He was also preaching on weekends in a small suburban church that welcomed his ministry even after he honestly shared with the church board his earlier indiscretion.

"The congregation really loves us," his letter enthused, "and the church is growing rapidly. I expect to be in full-time ministry again by the end of the year."

I also received letters from church officials overseas expressing their gratitude for the book. In one South American country an evangelist with an unsavory character had moved to a certain city, drawing people to his meetings despite warnings from some who knew his past. Copies of *True and False Prophets* proved pivotal in alerting Christians to the danger that faced them. The evangelist was privately confronted by several area pastors and given a copy of my book. A few days later he left town.

"We wouldn't have known how to handle the situation without your book," a letter from one of the pastors reported.

But in addition to the letters of praise and the letter of criticism—both of which I gradually learned to accept without too much reaction—other letters began to appear containing a question I came to dread. "We've heard that Rev. _____ has been involved in immorality [or dishonesty]. Can you confirm the charges against him?"

I even received letters with lists of names of well-known Bible teachers and evangelists instructing me to place an "X" beside the name of each one I knew to be immoral or dishonest.

Such letters became an agony to me. I fumed both to myself

and to God about them. Who did the writers think I was? Who appointed me sheriff in the Kingdom of God? Some of the first letters I ignored, hoping the writers would think their letters never reached me, but that made me feel guilty. Next I tried acknowledging their letters but ignoring the request, only to receive additional letters complaining, "You didn't answer my question. Is _____ a false prophet or not?"

Then slowly and reluctantly I developed a strategy for providing an honest—if not always adequate—response. If I were in possession of reliable testimony that the man named was guilty of repeated immoral offenses, and if the letter was from some responsible church leader or from one who had personally suffered from such immoral activity, then I furnished copies of what evidence I had with a strong recommendation that confirmation be sought from other sources. I was painfully aware of the scriptural admonition that out of the mouths of two or three witnesses "every matter may be established" (Matthew 18:16).

"Do not make any decision based only on your contact with me," I urged. "Check with other sources." Then, if possible, I would provide names and addresses of other leaders who had firsthand evidence concerning the offender.

Even more frustrating was the realization that while evidence against certain unsavory men was irrefutable, many were still in ministry because there was no way to bring them to accountability. When confronted by the leaders of one church, they would simply deny the charges and move to another area. In fact, the most brazen offenders not only refused to admit their guilt, they even claimed their accusers were in league with Satan and were deliberately trying to destroy their ministries. I recall one particular man with genuine evangelistic gifts who seemed to have supernatural demonic protection. A respected minister whose teenage sister was seduced by the man shared his personal story with me.

"I insisted on a personal confrontation with the offending minister," he recalled. "Four people were present at the meeting: my sister and I, the immoral evangelist, and the head of a nationally prominent Christian organization. Throughout the confrontation the evangelist proclaimed his innocence. When my sister described her seduction, he repeatedly interrupted, saying, 'You know it never happened; it's all in your mind!'

"Then he said to me, 'I have this problem everywhere I go! Young women become infatuated with me and fantasize about having sex with me. The devil uses their fantasies to try to destroy my ministry.' And when my sister looked him in the eye and said, 'You *know* you're lying; you *know* you took me to bed with you!' he laughed and said she just had a bad dream.

"Some days after our meeting he sent a letter to his constituency reporting that the devil had tried to discredit him by 'yet another false accusation' and that he had proven his innocence. But he hadn't proven his innocence at all; he had only denied his guilt."

Neither ample documentation in proof of this particular evangelist's dishonesty and immorality nor repeated confrontations by leaders in various parts of the country have been able to bring him to repentance or force him out of ministry. One woman who had been defrauded by him sent me copies of correspondence she had collected from various leaders whose help she had sought. All the letters she received acknowledged the problem and all were sympathetic to her plight, but none were really helpful. Here is a part of one:

Dear Mrs. _____,
     I have received your letter and want you to know I am doing all I can to have Rev. _____ send you the money he owes you. . . . We have endured much heartache as a result of this man's actions. . . . We recently learned he is living an adulterous life and has brought great agony to many people. . . . I am informing others who know him of his dishonest practices . . . he has also failed to pay me what he promised in regard to _____. I do not really know what else to do except pray and believe God to help you.

As of this writing, with the original *True and False Prophets* long out of print, we still receive urgent requests for the book, along with tragic letters from laymen and leaders alike involved in frustrating attempts to curtail the blatant activity of immoral men and women in ministry. We still have sorrowful conversations with confused and needy believers who have been seduced or defrauded by some tormented minister whose genuine spiritual anointing conceals a perverse, immoral character bent on victimizing the very people his ministry is designed to help. Peter's description of such people is blunt and unerring:

> With eyes full of adultery, they never stop sinning; they seduce the unstable; they are experts in greed—an accursed brood!
>
> 2 Peter 2:14

4

They Had
the Problem Then

Immorality in ministry is not just a modern tragedy; the problem is as old as the church itself. More than most of us realize, immorality and dishonesty plagued not only the members of the New Testament church but its leadership as well. In this chapter we will examine the struggle the early church had with the problem of false prophets, false apostles, false teachers, and false pastors or shepherds.

False Prophets

"Enter through the narrow gate. For wide is the gate and broad is the road that leads to destruction, and many enter through it. But small is the gate and narrow the road that leads to life, and only a few find it. Watch out for false prophets. They come to you in sheep's clothing, but inwardly they are ferocious wolves. By their fruit [not their gifts] you will recognize them. . . . Not everyone who says to me, 'Lord, Lord,' will enter the kingdom of heaven, but only he who does the will of my Father who is in heaven. Many will say to me on that day, 'Lord, Lord, did we not prophesy in your name, and in your name drive out demons and perform many miracles?' Then I will tell them plainly, 'I never knew you. Away from me, you evildoers!' "

Matthew 7:13–16, 21–23

It is more than coincidence that Jesus' warning against false prophets is immediately preceded by His warning about the wide way to destruction and the narrow way to life. His implication is clear. Some who assume they are on the road to life are actually heading for destruction because they are either false prophets or are the victims of false prophets. Not only that, Jesus says that part of the problem stems from the mistaken idea that a successful ministry confirms a right relationship with God.

"Lord, did we not prophesy in Your name?" they ask. But Jesus says, "I never knew you."

We could paraphrase Jesus' statement this way: "Although I chose you for My ministry, you were rebellious in your heart, and never manifested the fruit of the Spirit, which identifies any true minister of Mine. So I never approved of what you were doing. Away from Me, you evildoers!"

Evil in outward ministry? No, evil inwardly, in the heart where the rebellion and immorality lurk that identify the false prophet. In the day of reckoning, the false prophet's success in ministry will not excuse his immoral life. Every believer should be sobered by the realization that one may preach, prophesy, heal the sick, and cast out demons in Jesus' name, *yet still not be doing the will of the Father!*

Because we have failed to identify what makes a man a true or false minister, the church continues to suffer the onslaught of Satanic attack, even as Jesus predicted.

> "For false Christs and false prophets will appear and perform signs and miracles to deceive the elect—if that were possible. So be on your guard; I have told you everything ahead of time."

Mark 13:22–23

Notice Jesus did not say, "If you pray hard and take precautions, these things may not happen." Rather He deliberately prophesied they would happen. Note, too, that it is the "Christs" and the "prophets" who are false, not the signs and wonders. Moreover, the Scriptures warn that this will not be an isolated problem, but in the last days will emerge as a crisis of major proportions. "And *many* false prophets will appear and deceive many people" (Matthew 24:11, italics added).

It is precisely because the conversions, the signs, and the wonders that follow the ministry of the false minister are genuine, that Christians are deceived. Enthralled by the ministry—which is God's—they fail to discern the rebellion and immorality that reveal the true identity of the false prophet.

False Apostles

In the writings of Paul we find stern warnings against false apostles. One should read carefully all of chapters ten and eleven of 2 Corinthians for a full grasp of the problem Paul was addressing. He concludes his exposé with these hard words:

> And I will keep on doing what I am doing in order to cut the ground from under those who want an opportunity to be considered equal with us in the things they boast about. For such men are false apostles, deceitful workmen, masquerading as apostles of Christ. And no wonder, for Satan himself masquerades as an angel of light. It is not surprising, then, if his servants masquerade as servants of righteousness. Their end will be what their actions deserve.
>
> 2 Corinthians 11:12–15

Jesus spoke of false prophets; Paul spoke of false apostles. In His warning against false prophets Jesus said their message may be true and the miracles in their ministry genuine, but their natures flawed, lacking in the fruit of the Spirit. Paul tells the Corinthians the same thing about false apostles, warning them not to be satisfied with only the outward signs of apostleship. "You are looking only on the surface of things," he said (2 Corinthians 10:7). A careful examination of his total warning reveals the following signs that indicate the ministers preying on the Corinthians were false apostles.

1. *They sowed discord among God's people by discrediting Paul's ministry.*

> For some say, "His [Paul's] letters are weighty and forceful, but in person he is unimpressive and his speaking amounts to nothing" (2 Corinthians 10:10).

2. *They promoted themselves and exalted their own ministries.*

> We do not dare to classify or compare ourselves with some who commend themselves. . . . For it is not the one who commends himself who is approved, but the one whom the Lord commends (verses 12, 18).

3. *They corrupted the simple gospel with error.*

> If you receive a different spirit from the one you received, or a different gospel from the one you accepted, you put up with it easily enough (2 Corinthians 11:4).

4. *They were unethical in their financial dealings.*

> Was it a sin for me to lower myself in order to elevate you by preaching the gospel of God to you free of charge? (verse 7).
> In fact, you even put up with anyone who enslaves you or exploits you or takes advantage of you (verse 20).

Note that of the four accusations made by Paul against the false apostles, only one had to do with the content of their teaching while three exposed unsavory personal character.

So we find Paul denouncing church leaders who were both working miracles and teaching a high proportion of truth. (No false minister ever begins with more than a small portion of error, otherwise he might be found out.) Yet Paul identifies them as false apostles, deceitful workers, and ministers of Satan who were exalting themselves, perverting the gospel, sowing discord, and fleecing the Corinthians financially. Eventually, they would be exposed because true apostleship requires not only a godly message, but godly character. "Their end will be what their actions deserve" (2 Corinthians 11:15), Paul promised.

In Paul's first letter to the Corinthians we have ample evidence that spiritual gifts can function in a believer's life, even though the fruit of the Spirit may not be present at all. Paul begins his letter by commending the Corinthians:

> I always thank God for you because of his grace given you in Christ Jesus. For in him you have been enriched in every way—in all your speaking and in all your knowledge—because our testimony about Christ was confirmed in you. *Therefore you do not lack any spiritual gift* as you eagerly wait for our Lord Jesus Christ to be revealed.
>
> 1 Corinthians 1:4–7, italics added

If we stop reading right there, everything sounds fine. But as the letter continues, we find Paul rebuking the Corinthians for grave weaknesses of character, which include: 1) a bitter spirit of disunity (1 Corinthians 1:10–17); 2) incest (5:1–5); 3) fornication (6:9–20); and 4) drunkenness at the Lord's table (11:20–29).

Although Paul is not addressing leaders, the mixture of miracles and bad morals among the laity in the Corinthian church reinforces the point we have been making, namely that false ministers can manifest genuine spiritual gifts.

False Teachers

Jesus warns against false prophets, Paul warns against false apostles, now Peter warns against false teachers. In his second epistle he writes:

> But there were also false prophets among the people, just as there will be false teachers among you. They will secretly introduce destructive heresies, even denying the sovereign Lord who bought them—bringing swift destruction on themselves. Many will follow their shameful ways and will bring the way of truth into disrepute. In their greed these teachers will exploit you with stories they have made up. Their condemnation has long been hanging over them, and their destruction has not been sleeping.
>
> 2 Peter 2:1–3

The entire content of this chapter is given to exposing and condemning false teachers. In Peter's words we see the same pattern emerging that we saw in the warnings of Jesus and Paul. Although there is error in the message of these leaders, by far the greater problem is their unsavory character. Let us list the points in this chapter that confirm that the leaders of whom Peter speaks are false teachers:

1. *They teach heresy (2 Peter 2:1-2).*
2. *They are greedy (verses 3, 14).*
3. *They are adulterous (verses 10, 14).*
4. *They are rebellious (verse 10).*
5. *They are arrogant and slanderous (verses 10-11).*
6. *They are blasphemous (verse 12).*
7. *They are self-indulgent and gluttonous (verse 13).*
8. *They are boastful (verse 18).*
9. *They entice people into error (verse 18).*
10. *They are slaves of depravity (verse 19).*
11. *They were saved but have fallen again into moral corruption (verse 20).*

Note carefully that only two of the eleven points identifying the false teachers concern the content of their teaching. The other nine points identify serious weaknesses in character. That the false teachers were twisting the truth of the gospel is clear; but that their own lives were far more twisted is even more apparent.

False Elders or Shepherds

In Acts 20 we find Paul again issuing a warning, this time to the assembled elders at Ephesus. He tells them that right from their own number, false elders or shepherds would arise.

> For I have not hesitated to proclaim to you the whole will of God. Keep watch over yourselves and all the flock of which the Holy Spirit has made you overseers. Be shepherds of the church of God, which he bought with his own blood. I know that after I leave, savage wolves will come in among

you and will not spare the flock. *Even from your own num-*
ber men will arise and distort the truth in order to draw
away disciples after them. So be on your guard!

Acts 20:27–31, italics added

The Ephesian church has sometimes been described as the
model church. It began with the preaching of Apollos, and Paul
brought it into the charismatic dimension by his further teaching
and ministry. (See Acts 19:1–6.) During Paul's ministry elders
were raised up, whom the Holy Spirit Himself placed in positions
of spiritual leadership over the flock (Acts 20:28). Nevertheless,
Paul prophesied that not only would "savage wolves" come in
from the outside, but that also from among those very same
Spirit-baptized, God-ordained elders such "wolves" would arise,
preying on the church for their own selfish advantage.

We recall from Jesus' own words the kind of men those "savage
wolves" were: they were "evildoers" of whom the Lord Himself
never approved, despite their teaching and their spiritual gifts.
They may have seemed Christian insofar as message and miracles
were concerned; yet Paul said they would rend and tear the flock
at Ephesus by the selfish and sinful exercise of their ministries.

Repeatedly, then, we see the same truth reinforced: that the
conversions, the signs and wonders, the proclamation of truth,
even the fact that a ministry is God-ordained, provide no guarantee against a minister becoming a false apostle, prophet, teacher,
or shepherd.

So much for illustrating the reality of the problem. It existed in
the New Testament church; it exists today. Now let us examine
why the problem continues to plague us.

5

How Can These Things Be?

Matthew 22 records the account of some Sadducees who tried to trick Jesus with a fable about a widow who marries her husband's seven brothers, each of whom also dies. At the resurrection, the Sadducees ask, whose wife shall she be? Jesus' answer applies not only to the question of marriage in heaven, but to our subject of false ministers with powerful ministries as well. "You are in error," Jesus replied, "because you do not know the Scriptures or the power of God" (verse 29).

So many tragic situations develop in our lives simply because we do not know the Scriptures. To be ignorant of God's Word, Jesus says, is to be cut off from God's power. If we believe the Bible is the inspired Word of God, we are not free to say how God *ought* to work. We have a responsibility to search the Scriptures to determine how God *does* work, and then bring our wills into line with His methods and His purpose.

Christians often complain, "Why did God do this?" or "Why did God do that?" But it is rebellion that prompts us to ask, "Why did God . . . ?" while a properly submissive attitude will lead us to study God's Word, not to try and find "Why did

God . . . ?" but "Why God did. . . ." Only from a diligent study of Scripture will we learn the ways of God.

Let's state our basic problem once more: Why God allows a man whose personal life is a moral shambles to have a public ministry that is obviously anointed by the Holy Spirit. Let's examine five reasons why we have failed to understand how it can happen.

1. We have misunderstood the meaning of grace.

Far too many of us still stumble over the doctrine of justification by faith. We just can't believe that salvation is free; that we don't have to do something ourselves to earn it. We say, "Yes, I know Jesus Christ died on the Cross for me, *but* . . ." then try to add our good works to the price of salvation. Paul spent the whole of chapters two through five in the book of Romans trying to explain that we cannot earn our way to heaven. Nevertheless, countless millions of believers still struggle with the idea that they must earn their own righteousness. The problem often begins in childhood.

"If you are good boys and girls, when you die you'll go to heaven!" pipes many a well-meaning Sunday school teacher. So early on, we have heresy drilled into our earnest little heads:

> Good boys and girls go to heaven when they die.
> Naughty boys and girls go to hell when they die.

And the subconscious effects of that heretical teaching continue long after we've mentally accepted the doctrine that we are sinners saved by grace. We may even be able to quote the right verses:

> For it is by grace you have been saved, through faith—and this is not from yourselves, it is the gift of God—not by works, so that no one can boast.
> Ephesians 2:8–9

But while we claim to believe the grace of God cannot be earned, when we see spiritual gifts manifested in a man's or woman's ministry, we fail to remember that they are gifts given in response to faith, not rewards earned by good behavior. This brings us to the second reason we have difficulty believing immoral people can have powerful ministries.

2. We have mistakenly assumed the gifts and anointing of God are an endorsement of character.

Too often I've heard well-meaning saints say to faithful believers struggling to receive the gift of baptism of the Holy Spirit, "If you can't receive, there must be unconfessed sin in your life. The Holy Ghost won't come into an unclean vessel." As if by self-effort any of us could ever become worthy to be filled with the Holy Spirit!

It's the same lie we heard as children reasserting itself in slightly altered form: "Be good and you'll go to heaven" becomes "Be good and God will give you an anointed ministry" or "Be good and God will give you spiritual gifts."

But as with salvation, so also it is with anointed ministries and spiritual gifts—they are neither deserved nor earned; they are graciously given in response to faith. (See Romans 12:6–8; 1 Corinthians 12:4–11; 14:1.) Sometimes after ministering the baptism of the Holy Spirit or healing or deliverance from evil spirits, I have been embarrassed to hear, "You must be a holy man to be able to do that!" As if by some personal merit I could earn a powerful ministry; *personal merit has absolutely nothing to do with it!* Scripture makes that basic truth so clear! Acts 3 contains the story of Peter and John ministering healing to the lame man at the Gate called Beautiful. When those who saw the miracle jumped to the wrong conclusion, Peter quickly corrected them:

> Men of Israel, why does this surprise you? Why do you stare at us as if by our own power or godliness we had made this man walk? . . . By faith in the name of Jesus, this man whom you see and know was made strong. It is Jesus' name and the faith that comes through him that has given this complete healing to him, as you can all see.
>
> Acts 3:12, 16

Peter repudiated the idea that *his* power or holiness had anything to do with the healing. Why was his disclaimer necessary? Because the Jews back then, just like many of us today, mistakenly believed that a man must be some kind of super-saint to have an anointed ministry. Not so! Any Christian minister or layman being used by God in some powerful way may be no better morally than any other believer in Christ.

Although most people tend to accept an anointed ministry or spiritual gifts as proof of a man's or woman's godliness, the Word of God insists it is Christlike character, not anointing or gifts, that determines true spiritual status. Remember, Jesus said, "Thus, by their fruit [not by anointing or spiritual gifts] you will recognize them" (Matthew 7:20).

We need to recall the definition of "gift." Webster's dictionary defines a gift as "something voluntarily transferred from one person to another without compensation."[1] If it is a gift, then it cannot be earned.

If I give you $5,000, that gift says nothing about what you are or what you do. It does not say whether you are tall or short, strong or weak, hardworking or lazy, good or bad, wise or foolish. The only thing it says about you is that you are the recipient of my gift.

But that $5,000 says a great deal about me. It indicates that I am a man of some means; that I am generous and helpful. A gift says nothing about the recipient, but much about the donor. So it is with the gifts and anointing of the Holy Spirit. They say nothing about the character or morals of the men and women who receive them. Rather, they reflect the grace and power of God.

Years ago, a man spoke at our church who had been a hardened criminal before he accepted Christ. After his conversion he began to pray effectively for some of his ailing fellow prisoners. He testified to some of those healing miracles during the service at our church. Afterward, one of our ministers was very upset.

"How dare that convict talk like that!" he fumed at me. "The

---

[1] Webster's Seventh New Collegiate Dictionary, 1970, page 352.

very idea that God would give His healing power to a criminal is disgusting! Why, my uncle was one of the greatest preachers in our whole denomination and God never used *him* for healing. Yet my uncle was a good man all his life. How could God use a criminal?"

That critical minister failed to realize the miracles of healing were demonstrations of God's power and that they revealed nothing about the character of the convict except that God used him.

A woman once complained to me about a certain man in her church.

"Brother Harry claims he has the gift of prophecy," she lamented, "but he still chews tobacco, and when he's mad he swears at his wife. How can such a man genuinely prophesy?"

"I'm sure God would rather use someone who didn't chew tobacco or swear at his wife," I answered. "But if Harry is the only man in your church who has faith for prophecy, then he's the one God will use to bring forth His prophetic word."

In 2 Corinthians 4:7 Paul writes:

> But we have this treasure in jars of clay to show that this all-surpassing power is from God and not from us.

What does the treasure represent? The wealth and riches, the supernatural grace of God toward the believer. But what does the treasure say about the jars of clay? Nothing except that the jars of clay contain the treasure. Such precious treasure in such humble vessels, Paul insists, is a reminder that the power is from God and we cannot make ourselves worthy of it.

3. God gives and doesn't take back.

> For God's gifts and his call are irrevocable.
> Romans 11:29

Our failure to believe this significant little verse is another reason why we have failed to understand how the anointing of God could remain on the ministry of an immoral man. The word for "gifts" here is the Greek word *charismata*, the same word Paul uses to describe spiritual gifts in 1 Corinthians 12. This verse clearly implies that God gives spiritual gifts, and even if the recipient falls into sin and disobedience, God does not revoke His gifts. *Here we face a conflict between what man thinks God should do and what God chooses to do.* The understandable human reaction to this verse is, "If I were God, I wouldn't do it that way. If I gave a man a powerful ministry and he fell into sin and rebellion, I'd take the ministry back."

That would be man's way, all right. Pour out the power as long as the minister behaves himself, but the moment he steps out of line, snatch the power away! But we must remember, our ways are not God's ways.

> "For my thoughts are not your thoughts, neither are your ways my ways," declares the Lord. "As the heavens are higher than the earth, so are my ways higher than your ways and my thoughts than your thoughts."
>
> Isaiah 55:8–9

Our responsibility is not to try to change God's ways, but to *understand* and accept His ways. Psalm 103:7 says, "[God] made known his *ways* to Moses, his *deeds* to the people of Israel." Many of us become so enamored of God's *deeds*, when we see Him save or heal or deliver some needy person, that we never try to search out His *ways*. We need to say with David, "Show me your *ways*, O Lord, teach me your *paths*" (Psalm 25:4, italics added).

Our ignorance of God's ways includes the mistaken belief that God should give spiritual gifts as merit badges for good behavior. If that were God's way, then of course the gifts would be taken away for misbehavior. *But since the gifts and anointing of God are not given because a man behaves properly, neither are they taken away because a man behaves improperly!*

For God's gifts and his call are irrevocable.

As hard as it is for us to accept, and as hard as it is to understand, the fact remains, God gives His gifts and His anointing "for keeps." He does not call them back. Let us also remember how Jesus said:

> From everyone who has been given much, much will be demanded; and from the one who has been entrusted with much, much more will be asked.
>
> Luke 12:48

This should be a sober warning to any man or woman seeking a powerful ministry.

Can you see how our ignorance of the Scriptures and the ways of God have led us into dangerous waters? Many have assumed that the power of God flowing through a man's ministry affords automatic spiritual protection. Don't you believe it! The more powerful the ministry, the greater the danger to the minister. The more powerful the ministry, the more significant a target for Satan the minister becomes.

4. The ministry belongs to God and not to man.

Every ministry exercised in the name of Jesus Christ belongs to God; it does not belong to the minister. God says, "I will not give my glory to another" (Isaiah 42:8). We must learn to distinguish between the anointed ministry and the ordinary mortal through whom the ministry flows.

God will perform His ministry according to His wisdom, even though the human vessel through whom that ministry flows may not continue to live a clean moral or spiritual life. A powerful ministry entitles a man to no special protection from God. Rather, it exposes him to far greater risks than the average Christian runs. It is an unfortunate—perhaps even a tragic—development that so many starry-eyed believers jump to the conclusion that a minister is in some way "special," in some way more holy or more immune to temptation simply because God has anointed his ministry. But he is "special" only in the sense that God has chosen him as a channel or mouthpiece. God chooses us not because we are worthy, but simply because He loves us and desires to fit us into His divine purpose. "You did not choose me," Jesus said, "but I chose you to go and bear fruit" (John 15:16).

Scripture reinforces the point that God's concern for His ministry is one thing while God's concern for His ministers is another.

> As the rain and the snow come down from heaven, and do not return to it without watering the earth and making it bud and flourish, so that it yields seed for the sower and bread for the eater, so is my word that goes out from my mouth: It will not return to me empty, but will accomplish what I desire and achieve the purpose for which I have sent it.
>
> Isaiah 55:10–11

The picture Isaiah paints here is one of God initiating, nurturing, and harvesting the ministry of His word, which *He* sends forth. While it is true the Lord uses the minister to proclaim the message and minister the word, it is the message and the ministry themselves God is primarily concerned with here, not the obedience or disobedience of the minister. It is *God's word* that shall prosper, not necessarily the one through whom the word is ministered. God's loving concern for the minister we will discuss in a moment.

Even Jesus declared the ministry was the Father's and not His. He claimed no power of His own.

> Jesus gave them this answer: "I tell you the truth; *the Son can do nothing by himself;* he can do only what he sees his Father doing, because whatever the Father does the Son does also."
>
> John 5:19, italics added

> "By myself I can do nothing."
>
> John 5:30

And to the Philippians Paul wrote of his confidence that:

> He who began a good work in you will carry it on to completion until the day of Christ Jesus.
>
> Philippians 1:6

God begins His ministry through imperfect human channels and He will perform and finish His ministry through imperfect human channels, whether those human channels measure up or not.

God bestows a powerful ministry on various individuals, not because he thinks those particular people are morally or spiritually superior, but that the needs of His people may be met. It is *God's* love and compassion (not the minister's) that lead to a demonstration of *His* power (not the minister's power) to meet *His* peoples' needs. Once He bestows a ministry upon a man, that man remains His chosen vessel, even though the devil may succeed in wreaking havoc within the man's personal life. Remember how many times Israel rebelled against God and forsook His ways, yet they remained God's chosen people.

Now let us examine God's dealing with the minister, quite apart from his anointed ministry. We have already noted how a man with a powerful ministry is subject to far greater temptations than the average Christian. (I once counseled a former witch who confessed to me that she was admitted to membership in a witches' coven only after she had seduced three Christian ministers.) *A minister's position of unique privilege is also a position of unique peril!* The fact that he is chosen for an anointed ministry makes it all the more imperative that he stay submitted to the cleansing, crucifying work of the Holy Spirit in his own personal life.

Unfortunately, most Christians assume the lion's share of that crucifying work has already taken place, else God would have not chosen the man. Even more unfortunately, at times men and women chosen for anointed ministries fall into the trap of believing that they are somehow exempt from the kind of righteous living God expects from every devoted believer. Alas, both God's Word and contemporary experience confirm the fallacy of such assumptions.

It is for our own protection that God would have us understand that the marks of a true minister of God are not to be found in the anointing on his ministry or the signs and wonders that attend it, but in his character; in the fruit of the Spirit in the minister's life. It is precisely because the anointing and signs and wonders say nothing about the man that we must examine other credentials to determine if he is a true or false minister. As my friend Derek Prince has often bluntly stated: "If you want to know if a man is a truly godly minister, don't look at the success of his ministry; see if he pays his bills at home and if the woman he travels with is his wife."

5. God's judgment may be delayed, but it is certain.

The final reason why we often misunderstand God's ways is that God is so patient. His reluctance to pronounce judgment prompts immature believers to make all kinds of tragic mistakes. Something in our carnal nature wants us, when given an inch, to take a mile. That is, if we get away with something the first time, we will almost certainly try it a second and a third, or a hundredth time. As long as we feel we have escaped detection, all of us are tempted to appear self-disciplined while privately indulging ourselves. Against this tendency to self-indulgence and sinful behavior, we must acknowledge the certainty of God's judgment.

But God's reluctance to pronounce judgment is one of His divine characteristics that Satan uses with deadly effectiveness. Too many believers assume that since God's justice is delayed, they may never have to account for their sin and disobedience. This is a special temptation to the man or woman whose ministry continues to be effective even as he or she falls into sin. God's forbearance begins to be seen as indifference.

> He [the wicked man] says to himself, "God has forgotten; he covers his face and never sees." . . . Why does the wicked man revile God? Why does he say to himself, "He won't call me to account"?
>
> Psalm 10:11, 13

But the sinful, wayward man presumes too much:

For he [God] has set a day when he will judge the world
with justice by the man [Jesus Christ] he has appointed.

Acts 17:31

And there are many other Scriptures that indicate both God's
reluctance to anger, and the certainty of His judgment.

The Lord is gracious and compassionate, slow to anger and
rich in love.

Psalm 145:8

The Lord is slow to anger and great in power; the Lord will
not leave the guilty unpunished.

Nahum 1:3

The parable of the tenants, which Jesus tells in Luke 20, also
clearly illustrates both God's forbearance and His eventual judgment. It is the story of a man who planted a vineyard and rented
it to some farmers and then went away for a long time. At harvest
time he sent three servants—one after the other—to claim his
rightful portion of the harvest, but the farmers killed each servant.
Finally the owner sent his son, believing surely the farmers would
respect him. But the farmers killed the son as well. Jesus concludes the parable by saying,

"What then will the owner of the vineyard do to them? He
will come and kill those tenants and give the vineyard to
others."

Luke 20:15–16

Of course, the obvious prophetic meaning of the parable is that
since the Israelites stoned and killed the prophets, they will also
put to death the Son of God. But the parable is also a clear statement to the effect that God's forbearance in regard to wayward
ministers has its limits.

The owner of the vineyard is God and the farmers he rents it to
are the ministers of God. As God delays his coming in person, the
ministers, *still exercising their ministries,* become more dishonest

and rebellious, eventually resorting to violence and murder. It is important for us to see that one reason for the postponement of God's judgment against wickedness is that it allows all the rebellion and wickedness latent in wicked persons to fully manifest itself. The ministers shall eventually be judged and destroyed, *but only after repeated postponements of judgment, prompted by the longsuffering of God, who continues to hope for their repentance.*

> The Lord is not slow in keeping his promise, as some understand slowness. He is patient with you, not wanting anyone to perish, but everyone to come to repentance.
>
> 2 Peter 3:9

God's loving patience becomes a dangerous thing for a man entrusted with a powerful ministry who falls into sin and rebellion.

We have examined some of the reasons why Christians have not understood how God's anointing and miraculous signs and wonders can accompany the ministry of a man who is living a sinful life. Now let us see how men who begin as faithful ministers of God become snared by the devil and how the church's ignorance of the marks of a true man of God can contribute to his fall.

6

Why God's
Ministers Fail

At one time or another most of us have had the experience of
listening to someone discuss a problem so intimate and painful
that it can be shared only as if it were something that happened to
some fictional friend.

"I have this friend, see, and his problem is that. . . ."

Sometimes for purposes of clarity as well as privacy, it helps to
analyze and discuss real-life situations in such fictional settings
using such fictional characters. Especially with situations as unpleasant and sordid as those described in this book. So in this
chapter we will analyze two tragic, true situations, but place them
in fictitious settings.

The Case of the Reverend John Truehart

The Reverend John Truehart, pastor of the Newtown Community Church, appeared to be the ideal young minister. Married to
a lovely young wife and father of two little blue-eyed daughters,
he had met the Spirit of God in a life-transforming experience
while still in seminary. Upon graduation, he accepted the New-

town pastorate ready to prove to God and the world his dedication and faithfulness.

For two years he poured himself tirelessly into his work and the Newtown church thrived under his leadership. The congregation trebled in size from 300 to almost a thousand members. To accommodate the swelling crowds, the church erected a large new sanctuary in one of the most elite sections of the city. One of the most popular features of the church's life was a Sunday night prayer and praise service that drew people from miles around. It was a service where the Spirit of God was present with power and many people received dramatic help. Miracles of healing were regularly reported.

Young John Truehart was grateful but impatient. He felt God had called him to a much larger ministry and found it frustrating to live in such a small town where there was only a limited challenge.

Then a publisher became impressed with Truehart's ministry and commissioned a book to be written about him. When published, the book became an overnight best-seller and even greater crowds began to throng Truehart's services. He was also inundated with invitations to speak at other churches and conventions.

Of course, Truehart was delighted. He considered the book and the sudden expansion of his ministry an answer to prayer. He began to travel extensively and God honored his expanded ministry with large numbers of conversions and miracles. Almost overnight young John Truehart became nationally known for his ministry of spiritual healing.

But responsible elders in his own church saw danger ahead for their popular young pastor. While he was being touted publicly across the country as "God's man of faith and power," John's home church and his family suffered severe neglect. His parish work languished and his wife became depressed and miserable. While her husband traveled the country serving God, she spent lonely days and nights at home, changing diapers and struggling unsuccessfully to pay the family bills.

Those debts, unknown to the public, indicated a serious problem in the Truehart family. John had married a girl from a wealthy family whose parents had given her everything she wanted. Her extravagance combined with John's inexperience in money matters had resulted in their leaving seminary thousands of dollars in debt. And John's salary since graduation—despite the church's spectacular growth—had remained too modest to reduce their indebtedness.

John's new ministry and royalties from the book brought in some additional income, which he hoped would ease the staggering load of debt. But unfortunately, his wife's frustration and loneliness increased her extravagance and the Trueharts' indebtedness continued to rise. Of course, the churches and conferences clamoring for John's miraculous ministry had no knowledge of the crisis brewing at home.

Some of John's elders, together with two senior pastors in Newtown—all mature men of God with a compassionate concern for young Truehart's welfare—met with John between out-of-town trips. They gently but firmly advised him to curtail his traveling until things straightened out at home. They even offered financial assistance. John listened politely but insisted his responsibility to God and his ministry came first and that God would help him solve his financial and marital difficulties without their help. He also offered his resignation as pastor of Newtown Community Church. After all, he had been called to a larger ministry. His church accepted his resignation with regret.

"We really do want to stand with you in your ministry, John," his elders said. "We want to help you any way we can." To show their faith in his ministry the church board voted to continue paying John's housing allowance for at least a year following his resignation.

So John Truehart continued to travel and God continued to bless his ministry with conversions and signs and wonders. But the more John traveled, the greater the problems became at home. Creditors began threatening legal action and there was danger of public exposure of his private problems.

Realizing his wife and children were suffering from his absence yet swamped by continuing demands for his ministry, John fasted and prayed about his problems, but the heavens seemed as brass. Still, the anointing remained on his ministry and people continued to be healed in his meetings.

In fact, it was a dramatic healing miracle that proved a tragic turning point in John's ministry. A wealthy widow was instantly healed of failing eyesight in one of his services and no one was more humbled by the miracle than John Truehart.

The next day the grateful widow sent him a note expressing her gratitude and enclosed a check in the amount of $5,000 for John to "invest in the Lord's work."

"I trust you to send the money where it will do the most good," her note explained. Nevertheless, she made the check out in John Truehart's name. Satan's snare had been neatly laid.

The subtle process of rationalization set in. John couldn't seem to think of any work he felt was worthy of the gift. Besides, wasn't *his* ministry valid? And wasn't it *his* prayer that had brought healing to the widow? Weren't *his* debts and expenses as valid as those of any other ministry?

The pressures were too powerful and the temptation too great. In desperation, he deposited the check in his own personal account and paid the most pressing of his debts to forestall bankruptcy and disgrace. Almost immediately, remorse set in. He had been dishonest! He had actually embezzled money from God's work!

John fell on his face before God, pleading for forgiveness and promising that somehow he would repay the money. But beneath his agonizing prayer lay an even greater fear. How would his sin affect his career? Had his dishonesty destroyed his ministry?

With agony of spirit and sorrow of heart John stood up to preach at his next service. To his amazement, the anointing on his ministry was as powerful as before. *It was as if his moral lapse had made no difference in his ministry.* He could scarcely believe it!

But nothing had basically changed about his situation. His wife's extravagance continued to outdistance his income. He accepted even more invitations because of his need for the honorariums. Yet the more he traveled, the worse his situation at home became.

Then word came from the elders at home who continued to pray for John's ministry, even though he was no longer their pastor. John's wife had been seen leaving a cocktail bar at midnight with some "new friends," and a former parishioner had dropped by the house several evenings to find the children at home alone.

John raced home to confront his wife about her behavior and how it was threatening his ministry, but she was incommunicable and surly. One of his former elders firmly advised him to cancel his next few meetings. In anger, John refused. Instead, he hired a full-time housekeeper—which he could not afford—and flew to his next speaking engagement.

Once more his financial problems reached excessive proportions and angry creditors threatened to expose him publicly. This time there was no $5,000 check. Desperate for money, John shared with his next audience how he felt led to start a missionary work for children in Haiti. Over $12,000 was received in a special offering.

Significantly, John's burden to begin a mission work in Haiti was genuine. But at the time he had no program and no personnel for turning his dream into reality. The funds really were for Haiti, but it would be several months before they were needed. In the meantime, there were those angry creditors and those terrible debts at home. No one would ever know if he borrowed a few thousand dollars from the Haiti fund until. . . .

So Satan's snare was sprung and the Reverend John Truehart, dedicated man of God, became a *false* prophet, an immoral man traveling the country lifting large missionary offerings on the basis of his powerful, anointed ministry. Setting up a dummy missionary organization to receive the offerings, he maintained control of the funds himself through bank accounts in different cities. Contributing token sums to valid Caribbean missions in exchange for pictures and testimonies shamelessly used in his own promotional literature, he continued to divert tens of thousands of dollars into his own pocket in a fruitless attempt to prop up a disintegrating home and marriage. But it was all to no avail. Returning from one of his lengthy ministry trips, Truehart discovered his wife had taken their two daughters, moved back to her parents' home and filed for divorce.

The John Truehart Missionary Fellowship, Inc., may continue to function for some years before the truth is finally revealed, the ministry halted, and the dishonesty curtailed.

Were John Truehart's intentions to serve God honorable? Yes. Was his call to the ministry real? Yes. Were the conversions and miracles of healing in his meetings really of God? Yes. Did John Truehart begin as a false prophet? No.

Nevertheless, the point arrived in Truehart's life when he crossed over the line separating weakness from wickedness. A sincere man of God faithfully fulfilling his ministry, while struggling against a personal weakness, he changed into a deceived and desperate man deliberately defrauding the trusting, needy people to whom he ministered. Today John Truehart, by God's own definition, is a false minister.

The tragedy is that it was never his intention, nor his wife's, nor the church's, nor the public's, nor God's, that he should become a false minister. He was caught in Satan's snare.

The Case of the Reverend Randolph Abbott, D.D.

For twenty years, the Reverend Randolph Abbott had been pastor of a prominent 2,000-member church of a mainline denomination in a large midwestern city. He was past president of his denomination's annual convention and held two honorary doctor's degrees. For over a decade he had conducted a popular weekly radio program and was known throughout the city as "the radio preacher." Outwardly, Reverend Abbott was an imminently successful clergyman; but inwardly, he was miserable. Fed up with professionalism and with programs that produced little in the way of lasting spiritual results, he was desperately seeking more spiritual reality in his life.

Suddenly, things changed. Abbott's wife, a semi-invalid for many years, was miraculously healed when some Christian friends prayed for her. Shortly afterward, Abbott himself, rejoicing over his wife's healing, received the baptism in the Holy Spirit. Immediately, his preaching took on new power and vigor and both his church and his radio ministry began to grow at a remarkable rate. But some other denominational ministers in the city, envious of his success, began to publicly disparage Abbott's "Pentecostalism." When conservative members of Abbott's church learned the source of their pastor's new-found power and eloquence, they were shocked and demanded the truth from Abbott. Was he "Pentecostal"?

In response, Abbott testified to his experience during a Sunday morning service. That same Sunday night, the church board voted unanimously to discharge him.

Stunned and hurt, Abbott was making plans to leave the city when loyal friends who had been blessed by his ministry encouraged him to stay. So Randolph Abbott agreed to continue his popular radio broadcasts. A few weeks later he announced on the air that he was beginning a new church with no denominational affiliation. As he continued to teach about the supernatural gifts and ministries of the Holy Spirit, miracles of healing came to some who listened to his radio broadcasts. Surprised and emboldened by the new anointing on his ministry, Abbott began to pray regularly for the sick, both over the radio and in his new church. The new congregation—which began with a few families meeting in Abbott's living room on Sunday night—quickly grew to several hundred members meeting in a rented high school auditorium on Sunday mornings as God honored Abbott's ministry with a flood of signs and wonders.

Syndication of his radio program enabled other cities across the country to appropriate his ministry and within a few months he was also on television. Suddenly, Abbott found himself head of a burgeoning corporation, which made and sold records and tapes of his sermons and published books containing his messages. Some retired minister friends plus some sympathetic members of his former church served on the board of his new religious corporation.

"I thought when I was dismissed by my church that my career was practically over," he told them. "But now I see that God was just setting me free for a nationwide ministry."

But while his public ministry could not be faulted, Abbott, like all ministers of God, struggled with certain personal problems and against certain personal weaknesses. One was especially debilitating for him. All his adult life he had struggled against sexual lust. The years of his wife's semi-invalidism had proved an almost unbearable strain, even though he had remained faithful to her. After her healing, Abbott had expected a return to a normal marriage relationship, but to his dismay, his wife showed no interest in sex. Thus, his frustration grew even greater.

The first step toward his fall came during a series of radio talks he gave on the subject of "Making Marriage Work." His biblical insights into problem marriages triggered a flood of requests for personal counseling, mostly from women. As he met with one lovely young divorcée who came to his office for help, it happened. Abbott committed adultery. Reeling with shame and filled with remorse, Randolph Abbott threw himself on the mercy of God, asking forgiveness and promising God he would never see the woman again. He wondered if his total ministry would be lost because of this single trangression. *But to his amazement, there was no perceptible change in his ministry.* People continued to receive the same miraculous help as before.

Unfortunately, while Abbott sought desperately to keep his word to God, the young divorcée who had shared in the adulterous encounter began calling him constantly on the telephone, begging to see him. For some weeks Abbott refused. But finally, his will battered by the continuing temptation and frustrated by the frigidity of his own wife, Abbott renewed the affair. His public ministry and his public image remained unchanged.

But some of the ministers who worked closely with Abbott became concerned after he was seen publicly with the young divorcée on several occasions. When privately confronted by his co-workers, Abbott steadfastly claimed he was innocent of any wrongdoing—that his relationship to the divorcée was merely that of counselor.

Then, to Abbott's surprise, his wife received the baptism in the Holy Spirit. Her new experience in Christ rekindled her love for her husband and she became eager and willing to restore the normal marriage relationship Abbott had formerly sought. But now, deeply involved in adultery and riddled with guilt, Abbott could not respond to his wife's resurging affections. When Mrs. Abbott sought counseling from one of Abbott's fellow ministers, he reluctantly admitted there was substantial evidence that Abbott was involved with another woman.

Hurt and bewildered by her husband's unfaithfulness, she confronted Abbott. Tearfully acknowledging her part in driving him to infidelity, she begged him to break off the affair. They could begin a new life and ministry in some other state. Abbott rejected her accusation and refused to consider a move, citing his responsibility to his growing congregation and to the thousands of adherents to his radio and TV ministry. His wife then asked the men on the board of his corporation to intercede with Abbott in her behalf.

Lovingly but firmly, his fellow ministers insisted he temporarily resign as head of the religious corporation that had formed around his ministry, that he break off his adulterous relationship, and make every effort to mend his broken marriage. Once his marriage was fully restored, he could reassume his spiritual leadership.

"The Scriptures leave you no alternative, Randolph," his fellow ministers insisted. "We will stand with you through your time of readjustment and restoration," they said. "But if you do not step out of ministry for a season, we have no alternative but to make public your indiscretion. There is simply too much at stake for us to allow you to continue living a double life."

But Abbott refused their counsel, and angered by their "meddling" declared his intention to divorce his wife and marry the young divorcée. His intentions were quickly followed by action. Then he moved the headquarters of his whole enterprise to another state, and continued his public ministry. The thousands for whom he provided powerful ministry by radio and television knew little or nothing of his private problems. Abbott justified his actions because God was still blessing his ministry with conversions and miracles.

But word gradually filtered out about Abbott's unwarranted divorce and spiritual leaders in some communities recognized the dangerous path he had chosen. Doors of ministry began to close to him and some Christian radio and television stations dropped his program. Yet in other parts of the country his ministry continued to prosper with conversions and healings abounding.

After two years, a minister in Abbott's hometown was surprised when the beautiful young divorcée Abbott had married appeared at his office for counseling. Tearfully, she confessed that Abbott claimed to be receiving new spiritual revelations about the nature of male and female relationships. He claimed God had given him several additional female "soul-mates" and he had become sexually involved with three of them.

Moreover, she said his public teaching now frequently referred to a "new revelation for this age": secret truths in Scripture not formerly revealed, truths that would "bring the sons of God into maturity." Although he had not yet disclosed these spiritual secrets on the air, he was advertising new books that contained them.

"The most disgusting thing of all," his cast-off young wife confessed tearfully, "is that one of my husband's new 'soul-mates' came and told me she was pregnant and that God had shown Randolph and her that they were to be the parents of a 'new Messiah' and that his birth would be the Second Coming of Christ."

So Reverend Randolph Abbott's ministry continues, bringing blessing and healing to many who hear him, while Abbott himself becomes increasingly deceived and corrupt, having long since crossed over that fateful line between weakness and wickedness, even though in most of the country, he is not yet known or acknowledged as a false minister.

Were Randolph Abbott's intentions to serve God true and honorable? Yes. Were his long decades in the ministry evidence of a true call of God upon his life? Yes. Were his baptism in the Holy Spirit and subsequent increase in power in his ministry real? Yes. Were the miracles of conversion and healing spawned by his radio and television ministry genuine? Yes. Did the Reverend Randolph Abbott, D.D., begin as a false prophet? Absolutely not!

Nevertheless, this man is now a false minister, his grossly deceiving ministry a mixture of genuine miracles and tragic corruption, which will eventually destroy him and many around him.

An Evaluation

As we noted at the beginning of the chapter, both John Truehart and Randolph Abbott are fictional characters. I wish we could say that the incidents that led them into becoming false ministers were also fictitious. Unfortunately, that is not the case. *Every incident described is one taken from a tragic real-life situation—situations known to many of us in public ministry.* All I have done is link a few examples together with two fictitious characters for the purpose of illustration. And it would be easy to add additional incident upon incident of equally tragic nature.

Almost weekly, it seems we hear of some new tragedy or heartache surfacing in the life of some man of God who, extended beyond his resources and his protection, has fallen into Satan's snare and has crossed over the line from weakness to wickedness, from a true to a false minister.

In most cases these men and their ministries could have been saved. And in many cases, blame for their downfall must be shared by ministers and churches who choose to ignore that men of God can be trapped by Satan and become guilty of such behavior. Too many ambitious ministers and well-meaning churches—blinded by the signs and wonders and dramatic conversions—continue to invite false ministers for meetings and even hire them as pastors, although they may have been warned about their personal problems. Many of you reading these words—even if only by attending a meeting or giving an offering—have unwittingly contributed to the problem at least to some degree.

Now let us consider some of the valid steps we can take toward correcting this tragic situation.

7

What Can We Do?

The responsibility for correcting the situation we have been describing rests largely on two sets of shoulders. First of all, every man or woman in ministry should make every effort to avoid any snare that can trap him or her into becoming a false minister. In the next chapter we will discuss various steps ministers can take to protect themselves. But the responsibility does not rest with the ministers alone; an equal share rests upon those Christians in churches, house prayer groups, and interdenominational fellowships who are so hungry for the message and miracles of God they often fail to protect themselves from questionable ministries. In this chapter we will examine five principles that may help correct this unhappy situation.

Needless to say, it is one thing to recognize the dilemma and quite another thing to solve it. In all spiritual progress there is the inevitable lag between revelation and realization, between acknowledging the truth and being able to apply it. Nonetheless we can begin by trying to apply these five principles.

1. We must recognize that character—not anointing and gifts—identifies the true man of God.

The validity of every Christian ministry should be determined by the character of the minister and not by the effectiveness of the ministry alone. It is no exaggeration to say that most Christians involved in spiritual renewal become "miracle happy." We think nothing of driving two or three hundred miles to a meeting where the supernatural power of God will be in evidence. We long to see not only the lost saved, but the lame walk, the sick healed, and the tormented delivered from demons.

We are deeply grateful to God for the return of the charismatic dimension to the church for it was never meant to be without supernatural gifts and miracles. Nevertheless, such dramatic demonstrations of God's power can blind us to other important facts. Dazzled by signs and wonders, we may fail to exercise proper discernment about a particular man or ministry. Jesus himself warned his disciples against becoming too excited about the supernatural. When the seventy-two returned rejoicing because they could cast out demons, He said:

> "However, do not rejoice that the spirits submit to you, but rejoice that your names are written in heaven."
>
> Luke 10:20

Our relationship to God, Jesus insists, is more important than any particular manifestation of His power. While miracles prove that God loves us and will often extend His supernatural grace to meet our needs, they provide no proof of the Christlike character God expects in His people. We trust by now this truth has become abundantly clear!

A minister I know related this unhappy experience. An evangelist came to his church and people were saved, healed, and baptized in the Holy Spirit during his meetings. "Nevertheless," the minister sadly reported, "I sat in my church night after night and listened to that man make exaggerated claims about his ministry, exalting himself, telling lies that both he and I knew were lies. He seemed determined to mock the holiness of God and the sacredness of the ministry."

Equally tragic, according to the minister, was the indifference of his own elders to the problem. Awed by the spectacular ministry, they seemed deaf to the blatant lies and self-exaltation pouring from the evangelist's lips.

"I don't care if that man can raise the dead," the minister grimly concluded. "I will never again allow him to disgrace my pulpit."

Let us say it again. Signs and wonders, which may accompany a person's ministry, are no verification of his character. Let us thank God for *His* miracles, but then let us look past them and say, "Now what about this man? Is he truly a man of God? Is the fruit of the Spirit evident in his life?"

Neither should a minister be endorsed simply because he can preach an eloquent, scriptural message. The message, like the miracle, is God's. A pure word can come through a perverted mouthpiece. What's more, a perverted mouthpiece may give a pure initial message in order to prepare unsuspecting hearers for heretical teaching later on.

2. Every ministry should be in submission to proper spiritual authority.

As we seek to find answers to the problem of immoral Christian leaders moving unchecked across the Body of Christ and preying on its members, one thing should become increasingly clear. There can be no lasting purity, holiness, or order in the church without recognition of and submission to legitimate spiritual authority. Submission to delegated spiritual authority, mentioned so frequently in the Scriptures, means recognizing the legitimate authorities God has placed in the world and in the church, and obeying them as one would obey God Himself.

Unfortunately, the Body of Christ has reveled so long in an almost total lack of restraint that any mention of authority—let alone any legitimate exercise of it—raises the rebellious hackles of believers everywhere.

"Bless God, I serve the Lord Jesus Christ! No man is going to tell *me* what to do!" has become almost a nationwide cry. Perhaps we need to reevaluate such boasting. We may simply be declaring our rebellion rather than defending our freedom. The church has largely failed to understand that on earth God governs by delegated authority, by authorities He has set in place! Scripture teaches us unequivocally that all delegated authorities—kings, governors, traffic policemen, church pastors and elders, husbands and parents—represent the authority of God and are to be not only respected but honored and obeyed. Here are just a few Scriptures that illustrate the point.

> Everyone must submit himself to the governing authorities, for there is no authority except that which God has established .... Consequently, he who rebels against the authority is rebelling against what God has instituted.
>
> Romans 13:1–2

> Submit yourselves for the Lord's sake to every authority instituted among men: whether to the king, as the supreme authority, or to governors, who are sent by him to punish those who do wrong and to commend those who do right. For it is God's will. . . .
>
> 1 Peter 2:13–15

> Obey your leaders and submit to their authority. They keep watch over you as men who must give an account. Obey them so that their work will be a joy, not a burden. . . .
>
> Hebrews 13:17

> Wives, submit to your husbands as to the Lord.
>
> Ephesians 5:22

> Children, obey your parents in the Lord, for this is right.
>
> Ephesians 6:1

No issue in the church today is more fraught with emotion and controversy than the issue of spiritual authority. Almost every believer, it seems, has twenty good reasons why the Scriptures that insist on submission to authority should not apply to him or are somehow not relevant in his situation. As Bob Mumford observed, "In a day when lawlessness largely prevails in the Body of Christ, even the least application of authority is too much!"

For those who fear legalistic imposition of authority, we would point out that legitimate spiritual authority cannot be imposed, only recognized and submitted to. Note that in the Scriptures cited above, the responsibility for submitting rests with the one *under* authority, not the one *exercising* it. There can be no effective spiritual authority beyond a willingness to receive it.

Even those who demand the right to rebel against unjust authority should maintain a submissive attitude toward the authority, and engage only in "respectful disobedience." Submission is an attitude; disobedience is an act. So even when, for the sake of conscience and obedience to a Higher Authority, we feel led to disobey *unjust* authority, God still holds us responsible for maintaining a submissive spirit and attitude. In a sense, all submission to authority is submission to God and all rebellion against authority is rebellion against God.

The Christian activist who carries out a radical, lawbreaking demonstration against some unpopular or unjust civil authority may himself be rebelling against the authority of God. Similarly, the driver who disobeys the traffic laws of his community is also in rebellion against God. I can illustrate this from painful personal experience.

There was a time when I could boast of a twenty-year record of driving without a single traffic citation. Then, a few years back, in the space of six weeks, I was tagged three times. I began to suspect the traffic authorities in my community were out to get me! Each time I grudgingly paid the fine, but with only superficial grace. Inwardly, I was resentful. Why were the traffic cops out to get me? Why weren't they looking for real criminals instead of picking on law-abiding citizens? In my self-justification I conveniently ignored the fact that I had truly been guilty on all three counts.

Then I received a fourth citation and had my driver's license suspended for a period of thirty days. With that, I stopped trying to justify myself and asked God what He was trying to show me through the whole unpleasant experience.

And He did. It was rebellion. It was as if He said, "You claim to be in submission to Me yet you repeatedly disobey the authorities I have placed in your community for your protection." The thirty days I could not drive my car placed a huge exclamation point at the end of His message! Ever since that day, when I see a highway patrol car or a motorcycle policeman, I try to remember, "There goes 'God's servant to do me good' " (see Romans 13:4).

To be in submission to God's authority, then, means we must also recognize and submit to all the delegated authorities He has placed over us. Were all believers to take this admonition seriously and be willing to receive adjustment and correction from the men God has placed over them in the Lord, the plague of false ministers in the Body of Christ could quickly be eradicated.

3. We should apply the principle of plurality in leadership.

Linked to the principle of submission to delegated spiritual authority in the church is the principle of plurality in leadership. Simply stated, this means that no Christian has the right to say, "God has called me; I am answerable to no one else." Everyone should be answerable to someone. To *have* authority one should be *under* authority. Or as a wise teacher has observed, "If you are too big to be led, you are too little to lead."

Some years ago a group of elders in the Body of Christ had the painful and prolonged task of trying to deal with a minister in trouble. The man had exercised almost exclusive leadership in a work that had grown to considerable prominence and required the participation of many other ministers and teachers. Then serious flaws began to appear in his leadership, and a spirit of deception began to permeate every part of the work. But when other ministers involved insisted the burden of leadership be shared, the deceived minister became angry and rebellious.

"God gave me this ministry before I knew any of you men," he declared. "And I conduct it the way God tells me!" Only when his deception flowered into open immorality and became outwardly apparent to many people did leadership finally change hands while a shocked and saddened community went through an agonizing period of spiritual readjustment.

Once we acknowledge the need for plural leadership along with the need for spiritual authority, it seems apparent that no one-man ministry can be fully in the will of God, no matter how selfless the minister may be. Just as surely as God gives a leader authority to minister to others, God also provides other leaders with wisdom to guide and counsel him.

Scriptural leadership includes shared responsibility. God made this plain to Moses:

> The Lord said to Moses: "Bring me seventy of Israel's elders who are known to you as leaders and officials among the people . . . and I will take of the Spirit that is on you and put the Spirit on them. They will help you carry the burden of the people *so that you will not have to carry it alone.*"
>
> Numbers 11:16–17, italics added

The peril of large ministries based on one man's leadership can be illustrated with a geometric figure. Let us represent the man God calls to ministry as a cube: ☒

Even though he fails to share leadership, his ministry may grow into a great spiritual enterprise. But the result is a structure like this:

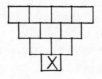

The whole work rests on a small, vulnerable foundation. If something happens to that one man, the entire structure collapses. From a spiritual as well as a physical standpoint, it is architecturally unsound.

Unfortunately, many ministries in the Body of Christ are built precisely that way. They are conducted by men who have authority over others but who recognize no authority over themselves. Most pastors have no pastor.

For every ministry, the wisdom of God would suggest plurality of leadership and shared spiritual responsibility. The ministry based on plurality can grow properly and safely. Structurally, it appears this way:

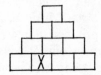

With a broad foundation of shared responsibility and authority, where everyone acknowledges he is answerable to others, even if one or two men fall, the remaining leadership sustains the work.

Let me hasten to add that the vulnerability of large "one-man" ministries does not imply that the ministers involved are false ministers. Indeed, most are dedicated men and women whose commitment to Christ is beyond question. Nevertheless, they sustain a weight far greater than God ever intended one man to carry, and too great a weight will crack any foundation. So then it would appear that all such ministries are highly vulnerable to Satanic attack. Inevitably the enemy will attempt by many subtle and powerful ways to tempt or deceive the leadership into making wrong decisions or taking some fatal false step. And once a minister falls into deception he is but a short step away from becoming a false minister.

4. We need to accept scriptural roles for women in ministry.

The role of women in the ministry of the church is a sensitive subject to say the least. Today, whole denominations are embroiled in controversy concerning the ordination of women. Some, like the Methodist, Episcopalian, and Assemblies of God have, for years, granted ordination to women. Other denominations like Roman Catholic and Southern Baptist still traditionally grant ordination only to men.

Obviously, the church is deeply indebted to the contribution of women ministers, regardless of the theological or scriptural implications of formal ordination. As I look back on my own thirty-five years in ministry I recall with deep gratitude certain godly women in ministry who significantly influenced my own life. Some were "faith ministers," like Sister Mittie Watters, known as "Mother of the North Carolina prison system." Friend and spiritual confidante to inmates and prison officials alike, Mittie left a promising musical career to share the love of Jesus Christ with "her boys" and "her girls" in prison.

Lacking any formal religious training, she overcame all kinds of obstacles to achieve hundreds of spiritual victories in a realm largely reserved for denominational ministers or institutional chaplains. A frequent speaker and prayer leader at spiritual life conferences, she impacted the lives of hundreds of young Christians, including my wife and me. During seminary days we became close friends with Mittie and, by her rich experience in the life of faith and her mature exercise of spiritual gifts, she added greatly to our understanding of the ways of God.

But our concern here is not so much denominational tradition concerning women's ordination—or even with examples of faithful women with effective ministries—as it is with what the Scriptures teach. And we need to keep in mind that Christian women in leadership can be trapped and deceived by Satan and become false ministers just the same as Christian men.

Scripture says that God has reserved a highly favorable, blessed, and secure place for women in His redemptive plan. In as beautiful a passage as can be found anywhere in Scripture, Proverbs 31:10–31 describes the cherished place of a woman in God's sight. Furthermore, Scripture plainly confirms the equality of men and women concerning their spiritual inheritance in the Body of Christ: their salvation and all the privileges and provisions that go with it.

There is neither Jew nor Greek, slave nor free, male nor fe-
male, for you are all one in Christ Jesus. If you belong to
Christ, then you are Abraham's seed, and (joint) heirs according to the promise.

Galatians 3:28–29, italics added

Husbands, in the same way be considerate as you live with
your wives, and treat them with respect as the weaker part-
ner and as *heirs with you of the gracious gift of life;* so that
nothing will hinder your prayers.

1 Peter 3:7, italics added

Both Paul and Peter make it clear that concerning our inheritance in Christ, men and women are of equal worth. *But equal*
worth does not suggest equal function. The point in question is
not inheritance or value, but placement and function in the Body
of Christ. While recognizing that many Christian leaders, both
men and women, hold differing opinions about how much weight
should be given to Scripture when discussing this subject, it always seems right to turn to the Word of God. On that basis, let
me list some of the ministries the Bible endorses for women.

a. *Scripture approves of women ministering spiritual gifts.*

Obviously, women were numbered among the 120 on the day
of Pentecost and received supernatural empowering along with
the men. Then in Acts 21:8–9 we read about the four unmarried
daughters of the evangelist Philip who manifested the gift of
prophecy. Paul also gives an indirect endorsement of women
prophesying in the church, provided they are under proper covering of authority when they exercise the gift. (See 1 Corinthians
11:5–10.)

b. *Scripture endorses women ministering in the company of their*
husbands.

Aquila and Priscilla are one such husband-and-wife ministry
team described in the book of Acts. They were tentmakers in
Corinth with whom Paul lived and ministered. They also traveled
with Paul (see Acts 18:1–3, 18). After Paul left them at Ephesus,

they encountered Apollos, a Christian teacher for whom they "explained the way of God more adequately" (see Acts 18:26). This husband-and-wife team is mentioned several times in Scripture—always together. There is no suggestion that Priscilla ever ministered alone.

c. *Scripture endorses older women teaching younger women.*

In the epistle of Titus, Paul tells us that sound doctrine includes teaching older women to train younger women.

> Likewise, teach the older women to be reverent in the way they live, not to be slanderers or addicted to much wine, but to teach what is good. Then they can train the younger women to love their husbands and children, to be self-controlled and pure, to be busy at home, to be kind, and to be subject to their husbands, so that no one will malign the word of God.
>
> Titus 2:3–5

I personally believe that the terms "older women" and "younger women" Paul uses can be legitimately applied, not only to women older or younger in years, but also in the faith. That is, a young Christian wife and mother who has years of Christian experience may often find herself in a position to instruct or train some other young wives and mothers who grew up without Christian parents and who have come to the Lord with little or no experience in how to make a Christian home or relate to their husbands or children in a loving, redemptive manner.

Moreover, as we travel the country together, my own wife, Alice—now that our five children are grown and married and have children of their own—is often called upon to share with women in the cities where we minister the insights and experiences she has gained in thirty-five years as a Christian wife and mother, a ministry in which she finds great satisfaction.

d. *Scripture also endorses women ministering care and hospitality to men who minister.*

Paul mentions several women who helped him in this way. For example, he said to the Romans:

> I commend to you our sister Phoebe, a servant [deaconess] of the church in Cenchrea. I ask you to receive her in the Lord in a way worthy of the saints and to give her any help she may need from you, for she has been a great help to many people, including me.
>
> Romans 16:1–2

Some scholars are of the opinion that since Phoebe was a deaconess in the church in Cenchrea, and since she apparently traveled from church to church, she undoubtedly conducted some kind of teaching and preaching ministry. While the Scriptures do not expressly say so, she may have. On the other hand, the "give her any help she may need from you" request of Paul could also indicate she was engaged solely in looking after the temporal needs of Paul and others. Many other scholars believe this to be the case. Whatever form her ministry took, Paul considered it highly important.

Before we consider some ministries Scripture indicates are not open to women, let me share a personal incident. Some time ago, while I was standing in the airport terminal at Muskegon, Michigan, waiting for the arrival of my flight, I noticed a small, twin-engine airplane belonging to a local feeder airline parked at the ramp. An attractive young woman clad in her airline uniform was struggling to place some heavy luggage through a door high on the side of the aircraft. With some of the bulkier pieces it took her two or three attempts and she managed the task only by straining high on tiptoe. I had to resist the impulse to rush to her aid and was relieved when a male employee finally arrived to help her.

As I watched her struggle it was as if the Holy Spirit impressed me with this thought. "Her problem isn't that she *can't* lift that heavy luggage, it's that she's not physically suited for heavy lifting."

That means she runs a greater risk of physical injury when she does it, I thought. *With his greater physical strength, a man can perform the task with no risk.*

Concerning placement of women in the Body of Christ, it's not that they *cannot* function in offices and ministries scripturally designated for men, but they face a greater risk of spiritual injury or difficulty if they do.

However, we should point out that many times when a faithful Christian woman finds herself laboring in a ministry scripturally reserved for men, it may be more the result of male abdication than female ambition. The late Kathryn Kuhlman repeatedly stated that God called her to a ministry a man had refused to accept.

Here are some ministries Scripture seems to reserve for men.

a. Scripture teaches that the office of elder or bishop is a male responsibility.

This suggests that women should not aspire to such offices, offices that have to do with rulership or government. Scripturally, such offices are held to be male responsibilities.

> Here is a trustworthy saying: If anyone sets his heart on being an overseer [bishop], he desires a noble task. Now the overseer must be above reproach, the husband of but one wife [not the wife of one husband], temperate, self-controlled, respectable, hospitable, able to teach. . . . He must manage his own family well.
>
> 1 Timothy 3:1–4

b. Scripture says women should not seek to teach if it puts them in a position of authority over men.

> "I do not permit a woman to teach or have authority over a man."
>
> (1 Timothy 2:12)

If the role for women in ministry is determined by the principle of authority, as Scripture seems to indicate, then for a woman to follow her own ambition into teaching or preaching to men means she must abandon her protected, sheltered role and assume a governing, authoritative role that may place her outside God's will and protection. Any minister, man or woman, who gets out of the will of God and who abandons his spiritual covering becomes a target for Satan's seduction.

c. Scripture says women should not seek to rule their own house-holds, even when the husband is not a believer.

> Wives, submit to your husbands as to the Lord. . . . Now as the church submits to Christ, so also wives should submit to their husbands in everything.
>
> Ephesians 5:22–24

> Wives, in the same way be submissive to your husbands so that, if any of them do not believe the word, they may be won over without talk by the behavior of their wives.
>
> 1 Peter 3:1

Notice that the admonition for wives to submit to their husband's authority is not based on whether the husband is "good" or "Christian"; rather her submission is "as to the Lord." In honoring the authority of her husband, a wife honors God. If she turns against her husband, she may be turning from God and exposing herself to deception. Many times I have sat in marriage counseling sessions where that was the problem.

Some time ago, a distraught husband sought me out at my home and told me this sad story: For years he and his wife, both Christian, had enjoyed a happy marriage. Then his wife seemed to grow restless with her role as homemaker. She began attending a women's group taught by an itinerant Bible teacher. Suddenly, she began finding "new insights in the Word" and began to speak of her desire to "serve the Lord more fully."

"She insisted God was going to give her an important ministry," her husband said. "I often tried to tell her that being a Christian wife and mother was a God-given ministry, but she would just shake her head and exclaim, 'That's not enough.'

"I knew something was wrong," her husband lamented, "but I didn't know how wrong until the day she confronted me with her 'revelation.'

" 'Carl,' she said to me, 'I know you and the children will not understand what I am about to say. In fact, God told me you wouldn't. Nevertheless, God has shown me my mission in life. He says I am to leave you and the children and become the assistant to the minister conducting our weekly Bible studies. I must obey the voice of God, even if it hurts you and the children. I want a divorce.' "

While there were undoubtedly other contributing factors, their marriage problems were certainly intensified by the wife's desire to have "an important ministry." Bent on forsaking her role as a Christian wife and mother, she probably had no inkling she had opened her life to spiritual deception.

I know some other Christian women who seem deeply committed to Jesus Christ and whose personal lives are exemplary in many ways, yet who occupy positions of spiritual authority over men. Their husbands are retiring men, nominal Christians who have forfeited spiritual leadership in their own homes and seem completely overshadowed by their wives. One woman even says God called her to minister only to pastors and other ministers since her ministry is too important for mere laymen.

But since such a position seems contrary to the teaching of Scripture—which forbids women to assume positions of spiritual oversight over men—it should come as no surprise that this woman suffers also from a measure of spiritual deception. She openly professes her belief in reincarnation.

Another one of the women teaches that since God loves everyone so much He couldn't let anyone go to hell, therefore, eventually, everyone will be saved. But both the doctrine of reincarnation and the doctrine of ultimate reconciliation are heresies in the sight of God, since both render Jesus' atoning death on the Cross as meaningless.

Are these women "false ministers"? All I can say is that their ministries are tainted with dangerous heresies that tend to make me pessimistic about their spiritual futures.

Does this mean that every woman in ministry is in danger of falling into deception and error? Not at all. Many godly women in the church are serving the Lord faithfully with effective teaching and preaching ministries. As we have already noted, God has every right to make exceptions. I agree with Bob Mumford when he says, "God reserves for Himself a sovereign 2%." Such exceptions should help keep us humble and from becoming dogmatic and legalistic in our faith.

But, in light of Scripture, I believe we should accept them and appreciate them as *exceptions,* remembering that exceptions do not invalidate principles. We should teach scriptural principles and allow exceptions, not teach exceptions while we ignore scriptural principles.

Any ministry conducted in deception, whether headed by a man or a woman and regardless of the signs and wonders that may accompany it, would appear to have within it the seeds of its own destruction. Many of us can testify to the collapse of various endeavors built on the ministry of men and women who assumed authority God never intended them to hold.

So while fully acknowledging His exceptions, let us thank God for the privileged, sheltered place He has reserved for women, and be thankful for all the sensitive, significant ministries they are called to perform under the spiritual covering of men in leadership to whom—according to a literal interpretation of Scripture—God entrusts the matters of church government and oversight.

5. We should accept and apply the scriptural principle of endorsed ministries.

Both the book of Acts and the letters of Paul make it clear the New Testament church leaders felt responsible for endorsing the ministries that circulated among the churches. In Acts 13:1–4 we read how the prophets and teachers at Antioch were instructed by the Holy Spirit to send out the missionary team of Barnabas and Paul. After many months of ministry, they returned to Antioch and reported to the congregation that had sent them out (Acts 14:26–27). It is clear Paul and Barnabas didn't just *go;* they were *sent with endorsement.* A group of leaders stood behind their ministries, accepting responsibility for them. Therefore, when their journey was completed, *knowing they were answerable to those who had sent them out,* they returned to give an account of their activities.

An example of an unendorsed ministry is found in Acts 15. The dispute between Paul and Barnabas on one side and the Judaizers who continually tried to discredit their ministry to the Gentiles on the other was referred to the council of apostles and elders in Jerusalem for adjudication. The decision reached by council was to be delivered in a letter to the affected churches. The letter contained a rebuke for the Judaizers.

> The apostles and elders, your brothers, To the Gentile believers in Antioch, Syria and Cilicia: Greetings. We have heard *that some went out from us without our authorization and disturbed you,* troubling your minds by what they said.
>
> Acts 15:23–24, italics added

In other words, the apostles and elders at Jerusalem considered the Judaizers to be acting without proper spiritual authority when they challenged the ministries of Paul and Barnabas. And because they felt responsible for the ministry they had endorsed, they were not only ready to defend it, they were quick to condemn any *unendorsed* group that sought to discredit it.

The principle of endorsement was also an issue when Paul and Barnabas made plans to deliver the letters. A dispute arose between them as to whether John Mark (Barnabas' cousin) would accompany them. Barnabas wanted to take him on the journey, Paul didn't. A violent disagreement followed and Barnabas took Mark and left for Cyprus on his own ministry trip, while Paul chose Silas as his companion on his journey. Apparently, the endorsement of the leaders in the church at Antioch was given to Paul and Silas, rather than to Barnabas and Mark.

> Barnabas took Mark and sailed for Cyprus, but Paul chose Silas and left, *commended by the brothers* to the grace of the Lord.
>
> Acts 15:39–40, italics added

We see this important principle in operation again when Apollos, a Jewish Bible teacher who submitted himself to correction and further teaching from Aquila and Priscilla, received endorsement of his ministry from the elders at Ephesus.

> When Apollos wanted to go to Achaia, *the brothers encouraged him and wrote to the disciples there to welcome*

him. On arriving, he was a great help to those who by grace
had believed.

Acts 18:27, italics added

In the writings of Paul we find frequent endorsement of other
ministries. In his letter to the Philippians he endorsed both the
ministry of Timothy (Philippians 2:19–23) and Epaphroditus
(Philippians 2:25–30). Additionally, he endorsed the ministries of
Tychicus, Onesimus, and Mark to the Colossians (Colossians
4:7–10).

But neither did Paul hesitate, when occasion demanded it, to
withdraw endorsement and support from false or fallen ministries.
In the book of Timothy he renounced Phygelus and Hermogenes
for rebelling and forsaking him (2 Timothy 1:15). He renounced
Hymenaeus and Philetus for heresy and ungodliness (2 Timothy
2:16–18), and he warned Timothy to be on guard against
Alexander the coppersmith who had plotted in some way to un-
dermine or discredit Paul's ministry (2 Timothy 4:14).

In his third epistle we find John withdrawing endorsement
from Diotrephes—a false shepherd—who, exalting his own ministry, had rebelled against John and was usurping authority (3
John 9–10). In the same small epistle he gave unqualified endorsement to Demetrius (verse 12).

So throughout the New Testament we find leaders heartily endorsing men with sound ministries and firmly withdrawing endorsement from the ministries of men who have fallen into sin,
rebellion, and heresy. From these examples in Scripture, we see
how evil, immoral men with false ministries could be swiftly dealt
with today if the Body of Christ could uniformly apply the principle of endorsement. If the leadership of every church would receive and endorse only the ministries of men and women of
proven character and integrity, and if they would refuse to receive
or endorse ministries that are questionable (either on the grounds
of false teaching or lack of fruit in the minister's life), not only
would many false ministries be halted and many false ministers
forced to repent and get right with God before they could resume
ministry, but the whole moral and spiritual life of the Body of

Christ would rise to a new level of purity and holiness. Surely nothing would make the heart of God rejoice more than that!

Unfortunately, such an ideal solution to the problem of false ministries is, at the present time, little more than a devout wish. Nevertheless, the principle of endorsement is scripturally sound, and its application can begin with each of us who recognizes its validity. In fact, regular opportunities to apply the principle confront faithful Christians almost everywhere. Hardly a month passes that some pastor or elder does not call or write to ask my opinion of a particular ministry. Often I am personally acquainted with both the minister and those who stand behind his ministry and am pleased to commend him. Asked about a minister I don't know, I simply admit I'm not qualified to answer and urge the inquirer that if he has doubts or reservations, he should seek diligently to find people personally acquainted with the minister, who can give an accurate appraisal of his life and ministry.

On those occasions when I'm asked about a minister whose personal life I know to be riddled with deceit, dishonesty, or immorality, *if the question is from someone in responsible leadership and not just from someone looking for the latest gossip,* I tell him I can neither accept the ministry nor endorse it for anyone else. I also urge the inquirer not to take my word alone, but to check with other Christians who can verify the facts. Frankly, such conversations are not pleasant, but they are an absolute necessity if we are to meet our responsibilities as shepherds of God's people.

An Important Word of Caution

Before leaving this chapter, let us admit that whether the problem is 1) recognition of valid ministries, 2) submission to spiritual authority, 3) establishing plurality of leadership, 4) scriptural ministries for women, or 5) the principle of endorsement, a real difficulty faces us, that of applying these valid spiritual principles in light of our human limitations and suspicions. One of the devil's favorite weapons—as we will discuss in considerable detail in later chapters—is the use of slander, libel, accusation, and character assassination to divide the body of Christ.

In attempting to deal with the problem of false ministries, we must learn to make room for one another's legitimate differences of tradition, and see that those differences do not result in broken fellowship, or in branding one another as false ministers.

We must also realize that some ministries, though valid, may not be universally accepted. A ministry that Christian leaders in one church or community may find helpful, leaders in another community may not be prepared to accept. To use a personal example, I am in the ministry of casting out evil spirits, commonly known as the deliverance ministry. But some Christian leaders do not recognize the validity of this ministry. In fact, by their standards, I may even be considered a "false" minister, while in most of the country, deliverance is recognized and my ministry is welcomed.

For another example, many theologically conservative Christians do not believe in the experience popularly called the baptism in the Holy Spirit. Some Christian leaders even believe anyone promoting the experience is a "false" minister.

So how are ministers with controversial ministries to function under such circumstances? Well, Scripture seems to indicate that local elders are the final authority under God to watch over the spiritual life of their flocks. As God's representatives, they have the authority either to accept or reject the ministries that come to their locality. Ideally, they should seek the advice and counsel of leaders in other locations but, in reality, they seldom do. So at times those faithful, responsible leaders make decisions that are less than perfect, walling their people off from legitimate ministries that could bring rich blessing. We must simply accept such incidents with patient understanding and pray for the day when all doors for legitimate ministries will be opened.

But as I interpret the principle, I am not free to minister in any church or community where the local leaders consider my ministry unacceptable. I must submit to their leadership as I would submit to God. To rebel against their oversight would be to rebel against God. It is God's responsibility to reveal the validity of my ministry to them, not mine. And until that happens, I have no right to force my way in.

In fact, at times I have been invited to come and teach with the stipulation that I not speak on the ministry of deliverance. Under such circumstances, I have two options: I can decline the invitation, or I can go in submission to the leaders in that locality and willingly limit my ministry in accordance with their request. Either course of action, it seems to me, is fully consistent with the principle of submission to spiritual authority.

In light of our different theologies and divergent religious backgrounds, are there some clear-cut tests that most Christians can agree will identify the false ministry? I would suggest at least three such tests that seem universally applicable. If a minister fails to meet any one of these conditions, I believe it indicates he either is—or soon will become—a false apostle, prophet, teacher, or pastor.

1. Is the minister known to be personally honest, morally upright, and free of deceit? Severe character flaws such as dishonesty, immorality, and deception are all blatant signs of a false minister.

2. Does his ministry exalt the Lordship of Jesus Christ and not himself? Teaching that contradicts Scripture, that exalts man, or that denies or diminishes the Lordship of Jesus Christ and his atoning death on the Cross, is a sign of the false minister.

3. Is the minister accountable for his words and deeds? Is he answerable to some delegated spiritual authority? Anyone refusing to acknowledge some form of delegated authority over his life is in danger of becoming a rebel and rebellion is a basic characteristic of the false minister.

It seems to me that every false prophet, false apostle, false teacher, or false elder mentioned in Scripture fails to meet one or more of these tests. Perhaps it might be a wise and prudent thing for each of us—minister or layman—to pause at this point and ask God whether or not we personally meet these three conditions.

8

Avoiding the Trap

In the last chapter we discussed at length five principles, which—if followed—could help churches and individuals protect themselves from false ministers. Now we want to list fifteen recommendations that the Christian minister, teacher, or leader himself can follow to avoid becoming a false minister.

Some of the recommendations are so obvious you may wonder why they are included. But sometimes the simplest answers can be overlooked and the clearest warnings go unheeded. A whole chapter could have been written about each of the recommendations—in some cases a whole book! I trust the brevity of the comments does not dilute their significance.

1. Ministers should be submitted to delegated spiritual authority.

> And we beseech you, brethren, to know them which labour among you, and are over you in the Lord, and admonish you; And to esteem them very highly in love for their works sake. And be at peace among yourselves.
>
> 1 Thessalonians 5:12–13, KJV

In the previous chapter we discussed the importance of delegated spiritual authority from the standpoint of groups and churches receiving ministry. I list it again in this chapter because I believe that submission to spiritual authority provides the greatest spiritual protection anywhere available for Christian ministers and teachers. In the verses quoted above, Paul seems to suggest that our ability to maintain our peace with God and each other is directly tied to our submission to delegated spiritual authority—pastors, elders, bishops, mature spiritual leaders—men God has placed in a governmental role in the church.

As stated previously, any minister who has not found and submitted himself to some form of personal oversight, which can provide not only encouragement but also correction, is in danger of rebellion and deception. For several years I was such a minister, traveling the country in blissful ignorance of my exposed and vulnerable condition. Looking back, I can see several occasions when, either through spiritual blindness, lack of common sense, or both, I blundered into situations of grave spiritual danger. It was only by the grace of God that I did not fall into Satan's trap.

But for more than fifteen years now, I have known the security (and sometimes the frustration!) of being submitted to delegated spiritual authority. I live and minister out of a covenantal relationship with three other ministers. That relationship provides the spiritual bond from which we each derive the right to advise, counsel, even correct one another. In addition, each one of us is under the personal spiritual oversight of one of the other three. While from time to time the responsibility for providing personal oversight has shifted among us from one man to another, according to where we may be geographically located, the spiritual protection and covering remains the same. Far from being a bondage (as some critics insist all such submission must lead to), submission to those three men and more specifically to my own particular pastor has proved one of the great blessings of my life.

Every minister or potential minister, if he desires to safeguard the ministry that God has entrusted to him, should find and submit himself to some man or group of men whom he can trust to provide spiritual covering.

2. Ministers should refrain from exalting or promoting their own ministries.

While a case can be made for publicity and advertising, every individual minister should exercise care in how he promotes his ministry.

> "For everyone who exalts himself will be humbled, and he who humbles himself will be exalted."
>
> Luke 14:11

> We do not dare to classify or compare ourselves with some who commend themselves. When they measure themselves by themselves and compare themselves with themselves, they are not wise.
>
> 2 Corinthians 10:12

> For it is not the one who commends himself who is approved, but the one whom the Lord commends.
>
> 2 Corinthians 10:18

No man given a ministry by God needs to bend himself out of shape calling attention to himself; for the same God who gave the ministry will open doors for the exercise of it. And the doors God opens lead to effective, lasting results, while sometimes those doors man forces open lead only to superficial results, frustration, and eventual failure.

It has been customary for many evangelists and Bible teachers to set up their own itineraries and plan their own campaigns. But as the principles of endorsement and submission to delegated spiritual authority become more widely applied, such methods, it is hoped, will become less necessary.

Even though a minister has been called of God, Scripture teaches that it is not enough merely for him to "go"; he should be "sent out" by someone and "sent for" by someone else. I pray the day may not be too distant when we will be so united with one another in the body of Christ that no traveling minister will feel free to exercise his ministry unless it is linked to spiritual oversight at both ends, endorsed both by those at home who send him out, and by the elders or churches who invite him to come and share his ministry. When that ideal day arrives, even local pastors will not only be subject to their own flocks, but will find spiritual covering under the authority and spiritual care of the elders of a town or city. Such an eldership will consist of all spiritual leaders of a given locality who recognize the need and are willing to accept responsibility for each other, leaders willing to spend enough time together to develop the degree of mutual trust necessary for joint spiritual oversight of their community. Such oversight will go a long way in eliminating the problem of the false minister.

For those who may fear that such oversight will lead to authoritarianism and bondage, may I once again add a personal word? My own ministry is carried out under this dual form of authority. I am submitted to spiritual authority in the town where I live and I never minister anywhere I am not specifically invited to minister. And far from being in bondage, I have a freedom and security in my life and ministry that I cherish most highly.

An exception to the principle of dual submission would be missionary activity and the establishment of new churches. In such cases, when a man or group of men feel led by God to go into a new area and begin a church or mission, since there is likely no one to do the "sending for" them, being "sent out" or endorsed at home would have to suffice.

But in this country, almost all ministry takes place where there are already churches and fellowships with established spiritual authority. In that setting, ministry under dual submission remains valid.

3. Ministers should keep their priorities straight: God first, family second, ministry third.

Many a man has fallen into Satan's snare and ended up in immorality or deception by getting his spiritual priorities mixed. In an earlier chapter we described the tragedy of the Rev. John Truehart, who allowed fascination with a powerful ministry to take precedence over his responsibilities to a young wife and family.

Too much ministry in America today is carried on at the expense of the minister's family. The failure of his elders and deacons to share pastoral oversight of the congregation has led many a sincere minister to neglect the needs of his family while he tries to get the job done alone. He may end up a successful pastor but a failure as a husband and father. A denominational minister friend once said to me, "I was taught in seminary that no minister who wants to succeed can afford to spend evenings at home with his wife and children; his church expects him to be out ministering to the flock or evangelizing the unsaved."

Those of us whose ministries require frequent travel away from home are especially vulnerable at this point. I know several fine ministers whose homes and families were literally destroyed because each man mistakenly put his public ministry ahead of the legitimate needs of his family. And this is not a problem for ministers only. Countless numbers of Christian businessmen have become "successful" only to discover the tragic price for their success was a broken marriage and children who hate or resent their father. The clear leading of the Holy Spirit—and not human zeal—must determine how much of a Christian leader's time can safely be spent on his career. Otherwise, his family will be subjected to pressures God never intended and the leader himself, under the agonizing strain of loneliness, will become especially vulnerable to temptation.

How, then, are a Christian leader's priorities to be ordered? *God first, family second, ministry or career third.* First, always, is our relationship with God. This should be true for every believer—minister or layman. Unfortunately, many ministers feel that unless they are putting their ministries first, they are not putting God first. But you can be so busy doing the work of the Lord that you ignore the Lord of the work!

In second place, directly after his responsibility to God is a man's responsibility to his wife and children, those who by God's own design have the primary right—after God Himself— to his time and devotion. But again, too many ministers feel that unless they are putting their ministries ahead of their families, they are not being faithful to their calling. Many a minister on the feverish merry-go-round of religious activity—if he could only slow down enough to hear God—would hear Him say, "It's time to go home to your family."

> If anyone does not provide for his relatives, and especially for his immediate family, he has denied the faith and is worse than an unbeliever.
>
> 1 Timothy 5:8

I personally believe that this admonition from Paul does not mean merely to provide food and clothes for one's family, but the love and companionship of a husband and father as well.

Two powerful illustrations of this truth are found in the Old Testament stories of Eli and Samuel. Both men lived to see the bitter fruit of careers given priority over the responsibilities of fatherhood. Part of Samuel's problem was that he grew up in the household of Eli the priest, who also failed in rearing his family.

> And the Lord said. . . . "At that time I will carry out against Eli everything I spoke against his family. . . . For I told him that I would judge his family forever because of the sin he knew about; his sons made themselves contemptible, *and he failed to restrain them.*
>
> 1 Samuel 3:11–13, italics added

Eli, a successful and faithful priest, failed in his fatherhood and failed to provide the proper role model for Samuel. Patterning his life after Eli, the man who was his inspiration, Samuel also ignored family responsibilities for the sake of his career. And his career was successful!

> The Lord was with Samuel as he grew up, and he let none of his words fall to the ground. And all Israel from Dan to Beersheba recognized that Samuel was attested as a prophet of the Lord.
>
> 1 Samuel 3:19–20

Nevertheless, Samuel lived to regret neglecting his family for the sake of his ministry. After a lifetime of faithful service to the

Lord, he watched the nation he had loved and served turn from the purpose of God, not because he had failed as Israel's prophet and judge, but because he failed as a father.

> When Samuel grew old, he appointed his sons as judges for Israel.... But his sons did not walk in his ways. They turned aside after dishonest gain and accepted bribes and perverted justice.
> So all the elders of Israel gathered together and came to Samuel at Ramah. They said to him, "You are old, and your sons do not walk in your ways; now appoint a king to lead us, such as all the other nations have."
>
> 1 Samuel 8:1–5

As God's chosen people, the Israelites were never meant to have a king; God was to be their king. But because Samuel failed to rear his sons in the fear of the Lord, Israel rejected the rule of God over them.

Such sober warnings in the Word of God should impress upon us the importance of keeping our priorities straight: God first, family second, ministry or career third. Only when a leader's relationship to God is right and only when his responsibilities as a husband and father are being properly met can he be fully faithful in exercising the ministry God has given him.

4. Ministers should encourage and serve other valid ministries.

In response to their bickering among themselves about who was the greatest, Jesus said to his disciples:

> "The greatest among you should be like the youngest, and the one who rules like the one who serves. For who is greater, the one who is at the table or the one who serves? ... But I am among you as one who serves."
>
> Luke 22:26–27

Some friends of mine were once attempting to counsel a brother who had been publicly censured as a false minister. They were advising him to yield to the judgment of God and give up all public ministry until his life showed the fruit of repentance and his family was properly restored. In the meantime, they said, he should throw himself wholeheartedly into serving other ministries.

"Would you be willing for a season to serve and promote ministries other than your own?" they asked him.

"Never!" came the rebellious reply.

Since one mark of the minister in trouble is that he insists on "doing his own thing," one way to guard against falling into Satan's snare is to graciously encourage, support, and—when the opportunity presents itself—serve other valid ministries.

The more secure a man is in the ministry God has given him, the more he will find it a joy to assist other ministries. Any man who feels threatened by other ministries or who finds himself unwilling to assist or encourage them needs to take a careful look at himself. He may find some root of pride or rebellion that may indicate a chink in his spiritual armor, which will allow the devil to strike a deadly blow.

5. Every minister should abide in his own calling.

> Brothers, each man, as responsible to God, should remain in the situation ["calling" in KJV] God called him to.
> 1 Corinthians 7:24

> But in fact God has arranged the parts in the body, every one of them, just as he wanted them to be.
> 1 Corinthians 12:18

Many problems arise in the body of Christ from the zeal of ambitious Christians who seek ministries and positions God has not called them to. Paul refers to us as members of one body. In the physical body, when a member is "out of joint," it causes a pain that affects the well-being of the whole body. So it is with our placement in the body of Christ. Even an effective ministry—out of place—will cause a pain in the body of Christ.

No man can be in the will of God as long as he tries to conduct one kind of ministry when God has called him to another kind of ministry. It would be a mistake for me to try to become an evangelist when God has called me to be a teacher. Nor does a man advance the Kingdom of God by trying to exercise his ministry in one place when God wants him someplace else. As Charles Simpson has noted, "If God has called me to a ministry in Mobile, Alabama, I cannot be righteous in Houston, Texas."

Most of us have met gifted people whose lives are full of frustration and who frustrate those around them because they are neither in the ministry God wants them in nor in the place God wants them.

Failure to remain either in the calling or the location God has chosen for us is a sign of rebellion; rebellion leads to deception and deception leads directly into the snare of the devil.

6. Ministers must be scrupulously honest in all financial matters.

> People who want to get rich fall into temptation and a trap and into many foolish and harmful desires that plunge men into ruin and destruction. For the love of money is a root of all kinds of evil. Some people, eager for money, have wandered from the faith and pierced themselves with many griefs. But you, man of God, flee from all this, and pursue righteousness, godliness, faith, love, endurance and gentleness.
>
> 1 Timothy 6:9–11

In the list of those characteristics that identify false ministers, greed and lust for money are prominent. False teachers, Peter tells us, are:

> ... experts in greed—an accursed brood! They have left the straight way and wandered off to follow the way of Balaam son of Beor, who loved the wages of wickedness.
>
> 2 Peter 2:14–15

Few Christians—either ministers or laymen—can claim freedom from temptation at this point. Since money is important to all of us, situations involving finances find us especially vulnerable to attacks by the enemy. Christians and ministers on regular salary may have relatively less difficulty in this regard than free-lance ministers whose support is drawn directly from love offerings and honoraria. Moreover, sometimes generous Christians unintentionally place an extra burden of temptation by the instructions they send along with a contribution.

A minister I know once received a check for $6,000 from a supporter who sent a note along with the check saying, "Use part of this money for your church and part for your own personal needs." How should a faithful steward divide such a sum? Fifty-fifty? Or, if he has great personal needs could he justifiably keep $4,000 for himself and give $2,000 to the church? In this case, the minister finally left the entire $6,000 in the church treasury, rather than make some selfish decision that Satan might later use to accuse him.

Then there is the matter of questionable fund-raising methods. Appealing for financial support is certainly scriptural and God's people deserve to be kept informed about the legitimate needs of the ministries they support. Nevertheless, some fund-raising methods raise some hard questions.

Is it ethical for a ministry to bombard its constituency with desperate monthly—even weekly—appeals for large contributions?

Can a radio or television preacher justify urging listeners supporting other ministries to redirect their contributions to him?

Is an appeal, which claims a soul is saved for every $4.50 contributed, proper?

How about the evangelist who sends "blessed billfolds" to those making contributions of $50 or more, billfolds that he suggests will assure the donor of continuing financial abundance?

How shall we regard the healing evangelist who stated publicly that God had shown him that no surgeon's knife would ever touch a family member of any person contributing $100 to his ministry?

Even granting that ministers employing such methods are sincere in their desire to serve God, it should be obvious that such techniques harbor a potential for abuse, which could quickly topple an honest work onto the growing heap of discredited ministries.

Equally dangerous is the practice of seeking wealthy supporters for a ministry. While professional fund-raisers have developed highly sophisticated and successful methods for securing the large financial sums needed for nationwide Christian ministries, the individual minister should be careful to guard his integrity in the midst of such methods. Too often ministers compete fiercely with each other in their attempts to woo wealthy contributors. It is an understandable temptation that needs to be resisted. Somehow it always seems easier to give attention to wealthy people who are interested in your ministry than to poor people who ask for your time. It was a temptation even back in Paul's day:

> Never once did we try to win you with flattery as you very
> well know, and God knows we were not just pretending to
> be your friends so that you would give us money!
>
> 1 Thessalonians 2:5, LB

While there are various legitimate ways of financing God's work, surely some ways must be more pleasing to Him than others. Jesus never provided us with fund-raising techniques, only with repeated assurances that God would hear and answer the prayers of His people. Surely, the safest and most pleasing ways of seeking financial support must be those that keep us the most dependent upon Him. George Mueller, head of the Bristol Orphanages in England, is said to have prayed in over one million pounds (the equivalent of $5,000,000) in his lifetime, while never asking a single human soul for money. Would not God be pleased to find a new generation of George Muellers in the ministry of Christ today?

7. Ministers should avoid extended ministry alone.

> The Lord God said, "It is not good for the man to be alone.
> I will make a helper suitable for him."
>
> Genesis 2:18

> Two are better than one, because they have a good return
> for their work: If one falls down, his friend can help him up.

> But pity the man who falls and has no one to help him up!
>
> Ecclesiastes 4:9–10

> Calling the Twelve to him, he sent them out *two by two* and gave them authority over evil spirits.
>
> Mark 6:7, italics added

A powerful safeguard against sexual temptation is present when men minister in the company of their wives. Even pastors of local churches who are regularly surrounded by their families may experience powerful temptation. Traveling ministers who experience lengthy separation from their wives and families are even more vulnerable. Many ministries wrecked by immorality could have been saved had the wife been traveling with her husband. Even ministers with young families can arrange some of their engagements so that their wives and children can accompany them.

The principle of team ministry is illustrated by Jesus when he sent out both the twelve and the seventy-two in teams of two. Also Paul, the greatest scriptural example of a traveling preacher, on most of his journeys was accompanied by at least one missionary companion.

The devil knows our weaknesses, and since ministers of the gospel are among his favorite targets, any man with an effective ministry will find himself from time to time faced with powerful temptations. But there will be fewer such occasions and they will be easier to overcome if he travels with his wife or with another man of God.

8. Ministers should not become overly impressed with the signs and wonders that may accompany their ministries.

> The seventy-two returned with joy and said, "Lord, even the demons submit to us in your name." He replied, "I saw Satan fall like lightning from heaven. I have given you authority to trample on snakes and scorpions and to overcome all the power of the enemy; nothing will harm you. However, do not rejoice that the spirits submit to you, but rejoice that your names are written in heaven."
>
> Luke 10:17–20

A wise older minister once said to a younger one, "God can work miracles through anybody. If he made Balaam's donkey speak by a miracle, don't get puffed up if he decides to work a few through you."

We should always be grateful for every demonstration of God's miracle-working power. But as we have repeatedly noted, it is folly for a minister to allow his fascination and appreciation for signs and wonders to dim his desire for holy living and righteous character. Remember, even false prophets can work miracles. Indeed, some who became false ministers were first lured into complacency by ministries that went on producing signs and wonders even after immoral behavior began to take its toll in their own personal lives.

So let us never forget that signs or wonders, which may accompany a man's ministry, are purely demonstrations of God's power, and never forsake a daily awareness of our own vulnerability and our need to walk uprightly in the fear of the Lord.

9. Ministers should keep their ministries scriptural.

> Do your best to present yourself to God as one approved, a workman who does not need to be ashamed and who correctly handles the word of truth.
>
> 2 Timothy 2:15

We live in a time of unprecedented supernatural activity in the church. Much of it has scriptural sanction; much of it does not. Not only is God pouring out His Spirit on all flesh with an astounding display of signs and wonders, but Satan is also producing an abundance of his own "counterfeit miracles, signs and wonders" (2 Thessalonians 2:9). Moreover, Satan also cunningly creates confusion by prompting the abuse of genuine spiritual gifts, as he did with the unruly Corinthians. (See 1 Corinthians 12, 14.)

But as Paul pointed out to them, "God is not a God of disorder but of peace" (1 Corinthians 14:33). The gifts of prophecy, tongues, and interpretation of tongues used in Corinth were genuine gifts of the Holy Spirit. But Satan, who is the god of disorder, was inspiring their improper use. He is a master at creating disorder and confusion in the ranks of God's people!

Not only do we regularly come in contact with sincere Christians who are misusing genuine spiritual gifts, we also minister regularly to gullible believers who have become deceived and captivated by weird experiences in spiritualism, fortune-telling, or other forms of occultism. When we try to warn them about such involvement they often protest, saying, "Oh, but it's supernatural; it must be from God!" Even though these supernatural experiences are strictly forbidden in Scripture, they stoutly maintain they are in contact with God. Indeed, one young minister who was cultivating listening to an inner voice told me that since he had the "Master Teacher" within, he no longer saw the necessity of reading the Scriptures.

"Besides," he said, "what makes you think revelation ended with the close of the New Testament? I receive additional revelation from God every day!" Already deep in deception and error, he would not receive the counsel I offered.

Paul makes it plain that the Scriptures themselves contain all the teaching and revelation needed for this life.

> All Scripture is God-breathed and is useful for teaching, rebuking, correcting and training in righteousness, so that the man of God may be thoroughly equipped for every good work.
>
> 2 Timothy 3:16–17

Revelation also warns us that any believer who departs from the Scriptures does so at his own grave peril:

> If anyone adds anything [or] ... takes words away from this book of prophecy, God will take away from him his share in the tree of life.
>
> Revelation 22:18–19

10. Ministers should strive to live under discipline and cultivate the fruit of the Spirit.

> But the fruit of the Spirit is love, joy, peace, patience, kindness, goodness, faithfulness, gentleness and self-control. ...

Those who belong to Christ Jesus have crucified the sinful nature with its passions and desires.

Galatians 5:22, 24

The manifestation of God's supernatural gifts often attracts huge crowds of enthusiastic believers. In fact, it becomes deceptively easy to travel from one miracle meeting to another, witnessing the demonstration of God's power while making no sustained serious effort at personal spiritual growth. In fact, many of the false ministries we have difficulty with today might never have arisen had it not been for an overemphasis on the gifts of the Holy Spirit at the expense of the fruit of the Spirit. Only by a deliberate and sustained emphasis on cultivating the fruit of the Spirit can the gifts and fruit be brought into proper balance. Essentially, it is the absence of the fruit of the Spirit that identifies a man as a false minister.

For that matter, the lives of most of us—minister or not—would be greatly strengthened if we gave more earnest attention to developing the fruit of the Spirit.

11. Ministers should strive for balance in their ministries.

For I have not hesitated to proclaim to you the whole will of God.

Acts 20:27

Paul was not claiming he had all the truth, but he was reminding the Ephesian elders that his teaching had covered many areas of spiritual concern. While no minister today would likely place himself on a par with Paul, every minister does have the potential for a well-rounded, mature ministry. Although each believer has his own particular calling or emphasis in ministry, that does not excuse him from striving to increase his understanding of the whole will of God. There is real danger in becoming too much of a specialist.

One of the ways an otherwise effective ministry can be snared by Satan is by the process we call "error by emphasis." Any single scriptural truth can become heresy if it is overemphasized in disregard of other scriptural truths. Some years ago a cultic group arose in the body of Christ claiming a revelation that made them a unique people. Some of their teaching even indicated they would not die. They called themselves the "Manifested Sons of God." In addition, their doctrine emphasized other legitimate concerns like 1) maturity, 2) the body, and 3) sonship. But when those doctrines are distorted by overemphasis, "maturity" becomes the privilege of an elite few; overemphasis on "the body" lessens the preeminence of Jesus Christ who is the Head; and overemphasis on "sonship" ignores sexual distinctives and the scriptural teaching on husband and wife relationships. The unhappy results included husbands and wives living as brother and sister, and women being installed in particular positions of leadership and authority that the Word of God does not sanction.

To avoid error by emphasis, every man ministering in areas in which God has already given him competence should remain open to other biblical truths and emphases. He should be constantly seeking a scriptural balance that will ensure maturity and increased effectiveness in his own ministry.

12. Ministers should stay in fellowship with other ministers and with other Christians.

> Let us hold unswervingly to the hope we profess, for he who promised is faithful. And let us consider how we may spur one another on toward love and good deeds. Let us not give up meeting together, as some are in the habit of doing, but let us encourage one another.
>
> Hebrews 10:23–25

A major safeguard for any ministry is *fellowship*. There can be no such thing as maturity apart from spending time with other believers. Separation from God's people inevitably tends to "exclusiveness."

Every valid revelation and every valid ministry must stand the light of Christian fellowship. I know a family in a certain city who withdrew from their church because the other members were "too worldly." As a result, this family became super-spiritual and began to invite certain selected individuals and couples to their house who were ready to receive new revelations that worldly Christians were not ready to receive. One of those "revelations" declared the Holy Spirit to be the female member of the God-head.

Seen in context, the verses we quoted from Hebrews 10 make it clear that part of the value of "meeting together" lies in giving us opportunity to encourage one another to "hold unswervingly to the hope we profess." Many a budding heresy could have been nipped in its infancy had it been brought into the light and examined in the midst of healthy Christian fellowship.

13. Ministers should be aware they are favorite targets of Satan.

> Be self-controlled and alert. Your enemy the devil prowls around like a roaring lion looking for someone to devour. Resist him, standing firm in the faith.
>
> 1 Peter 5:8–9

There is an old adage that says "forewarned is forearmed." The intensity of the spiritual warfare swirling around us these days demands that we be continually geared to a wartime footing. Each of us faces the same personal adversary who seeks, through the influence of myriads of evil spirits, to confuse, discredit, discourage, and defeat us in our efforts to serve God.

A major transition in my life and ministry occurred some eighteen years ago when I discovered the reality of the devil and evil spirits and began to actively oppose them. I recorded the effect of those events and my entry into the ministry of casting out demons in a book, *Deliver Us from Evil,* which I mentioned back in chapter one. I learned that we need not be intimidated by the devil, nor minister in fear of him. Rather, God expects us to be wise about his tactics and competent in Christ to deal with them.

For example, we need to understand how he always chooses the time and place of our own greatest vulnerability. We need to recognize how he often accuses us through our own families and friends. We will expose his success in that particular strategy in detail in the final chapters of this book. If, as Paul says, we are not "unaware of Satan's schemes" (2 Corinthians 2:11) and if we remain alert, we can weather every attack and endure successfully the buffeting and torment he will try to lay upon us.

> Finally, be strong in the Lord and in his mighty power. Put on the full armor of God so that you can take your stand against the devil's schemes. For our struggle is not against flesh and blood, but against the rulers, against the authorities, against the powers of this dark world and against the spiritual forces of evil in the heavenly realms.
>
> Ephesians 6:10–12

14. Ministers should be sensitive to what God is saying to the whole body of Christ.

> Where no counsel is, the people fall: but in the multitude of counsellors there is safety.
>
> Proverbs 11:14, KJV

> "For who has known the mind of the Lord that he may instruct him?" But *we* [not I] have the mind of Christ.
>
> 1 Corinthians 2:16, italics added

Can any man say, "*I* have the mind of Christ" and be totally correct? Truth is meant for the whole body of believers. Although the initial revelation may begin with one man or a small group of men, God will soon quicken it to a larger portion of the body of Christ. Therefore, any private revelation should be able to stand scrutiny, first by mature leaders and later by the larger group. Moreover, every minister needs to be sensitive to what the Holy Spirit is saying to the rest of the body of Christ. Revelation is strengthened when responsible leaders in various parts of the country confirm it and begin to proclaim it together as truth.

> Surely the Sovereign Lord does nothing without revealing his plan to his servants the prophets.
>
> Amos 3:7

Notice that God's revelation is not given to *a* prophet but to *the prophets*. Therefore, if a minister's "new revelation" is not quickly confirmed by a portion of the responsible leadership of the body of Christ, he should keep it to himself or drop it altogether.

15. Ministers should avoid rapid advance in ministry.

> "His master replied, 'Well done, good and faithful servant! You have been faithful with a few things; I will put you in charge of many things.' "
>
> Matthew 25:21

> Now the overseer must be above reproach. . . . He must not be a recent convert, or he may become conceited and fall under the same judgment as the devil.
>
> 1 Timothy 3:2, 6

Nowhere is an understanding of the principle of spiritual growth needed more these days than within the Christian ministry itself. In a time of spectacular spiritual breakthrough and burgeoning signs and wonders, the seeds of ministerial downfall are easily sown. For some impulsive Christians, it often proves a time of "too much too soon."

By means of some miracle or dramatic conversion, many a novice Christian is suddenly vaulted into public view. He finds himself speaking in large conferences and being interviewed on radio and television. Often enthusiastic followers encourage him to accept some position of spiritual influence or leadership he is not mature enough to handle. The result is often tragic.

I remember quite vividly the young minister—a former rock musician who had been dramatically converted—who addressed an audience of about 150 people with these sarcastic words: "I suppose God is trying to teach me a lesson in humility! This is the first time in my public ministry I have ever had to address a congregation of fewer than five hundred people." Could it be that the young man's meteoric rise in Christian circles resulted in more than a little spiritual pride?

If Moses spent forty years on the back side of the desert before he was equipped to minister, if Jesus spent His first thirty years in His father's carpenter shop, why all the rush? Seasoned, proven ministries are essential to the fulfillment of God's purposes today. Public ministry is so fraught with danger, even for mature men of God, the novice is almost certain to fall prey to some enticing dishonesty or shameful immorality if he gets too much public exposure too soon.

Every new and unproven ministry should be securely linked and safely submitted to older, proven ministries for a time of apprenticeship. Without such a period of training and seasoning, no young minister—regardless of his gifts—has much chance for long-term survival.

9

How Firm
a Foundation?

In the closing verses of the Sermon on the Mount Jesus gives a warning about false prophets that is far more sober and pertinent than many believers have realized. After declaring that even "evildoers" can perform miracles by the power of God, He adds:

> "Therefore everyone who hears these words of mine and puts them into practice is like a wise man who built his house on the rock. The rain came down, the streams rose, and the winds blew and beat against that house; yet it did not fall, because it had its foundation on the rock. But everyone who hears these words of mine and does not put them into practice is like a foolish man who built his house on sand. The rain came down, the streams rose, and the winds blew and beat against that house, and it fell with a great crash."
>
> Matthew 7:24–27

The initial meaning of this parable seems obvious enough; it is wise to obey the word of the Lord and foolish to disobey the word of the Lord. But when we examine it more closely, we begin to see how strikingly relevant it is to the subject of false ministers. More than that, the parable reveals why it is often so difficult for us to distinguish between the true minister and the false minister. The following five comparisons between the wise man and the foolish man will illustrate what I mean.

Both the wise man and the foolish man are called to build.

Obviously, both men had the calling to be carpenters since it takes a carpenter to build a house. However, there is no indication from their calling how either man will turn out: wise or foolish, true or false. Both are simply identified as builders or carpenters.

Both the wise man and the foolish man fulfilled their calling.

From the parable we learn that both men worked to fulfill their calling. Each one built a house. Even though it later turns out that one carpenter was a wise builder and one carpenter a foolish builder, or—to apply the story to our subject—that one was a true minister and one a false minister, the fact remains that both men built houses. In the same way the false minister can exercise his ministry just as fully as the true minister exercises his. Both may be diligent in fulfilling their callings.

The house the wise man built and the house the foolish man built may well have been identical.

In Jesus' teaching there is no hint of any difference in the construction of the two houses. The carpenters may even have used identical blueprints to build beautiful, spacious, *identical* homes.

So it is with the true and the false minister. Regarding the exercise of their ministries, there may be no outward difference at all. Both may teach and preach effectively; both may be known for their ability to help people; both may have signs and wonders attesting to the validity of their message.

The house the wise man built and the house the foolish man built may furnish exactly the same shelter and comfort.

Just as the two houses may be the same in size and appearance, so they may also be identical on the inside. They may have been furnished with the same furniture and may have provided the same shelter and comfort to those taking refuge under their roofs. So it may be with the ministries conducted by the true and the false minister. Both ministries may provide great blessing and comfort to those who receive them. A man converted to Jesus Christ or healed by the power of God under the ministry of a false minister is just as converted and just as healed as he would be under the ministry of a true minister. (Remember our earlier observation that the ministry belongs to God and not the man!) As we have repeatedly stated, genuine miracles of God can flow through the ministries of both true and false ministers.

Now, if I haven't lost you by taking the analogy this far, stay with me just one more step.

Both the house the wise man built and the house the foolish man built are subject to the wind and the rain.

"What," you may ask, "does that have to do with anything?" Simply this: both wind and rain are symbols of the Holy Spirit in Scripture. There is the "early rain," which many biblical scholars believe refers to the original outpouring of the Holy Spirit at Pentecost, and the "latter rain," which they believe refers to the current charismatic renewal in the church. And the word for "wind" (*pneuma*) is the same as the word for "breath" or "spirit" in New Testament Greek.

The parable states that both houses are subject to the wind and the rain. So also are the works and ministries of the true and false minister subject to the outpouring of the Holy Spirit. Rather startling to consider, isn't it? There are such similarities, no wonder the devil has been so successful in seducing and deceiving the saints! You almost end up wondering how anyone can ever tell the difference between the wise and foolish man, or the true and false minister. We'll discuss that further, but first let us review the identical features once more.

1. Both the wise and the foolish man are called to be builders just as the true and false ministers are called to be ministers.

2. Both builders fulfill their calling and build houses just as both ministers fulfill their callings and minister to the people of God.

3. The house built by the foolish builder may be identical to the house built by the wise builder, just as the ministry of the false minister may be identical to the ministry of the true minister.

4. The house built by the foolish builder and the house built by the wise builder may provide the same shelter and comfort, just as the ministry of the false minister and the ministry of the true ministry may provide the same blessings and miracles.

5. Both the house built by the foolish builder and the house built by the wise builder encounter the wind and the rain, just as both the ministry of the false minister and the ministry of the true minister encounter the supernatural power of the Holy Spirit. In this final similarity we find the answer to our dilemma.

We pointed out in an earlier chapter that to have a powerful ministry is to occupy not only a position of great privilege, but also a position of great peril. This parable graphically illustrates that truth.

Let a rainstorm and a windstorm continue long enough and strong enough and what happens? A flood—even a hurricane— results. And in Jesus' parable that storm accomplishes two things. First of all, it exposes the contrasting foundations on which the two identical houses were built. The wind and rain striking against the foundation of the wise builder's house reveal the solidity of the rock on which it is built. The wise man's house stands firm. But the same wind and rain striking against the foundation of the foolish builder's house reveal a house built on a faulty foundation. The rising wind and water from the storm eventually erode the sandy foundation and the house crashes in on itself.

Now we can foresee the final end of the ministries of the true and false ministers. Both ministers—in fulfillment of their callings—may have established identical works, equally powerful and effective. But when the full flood of the Holy Spirit rises, when the full force of God's heavenly wind is experienced, it will be revealed that one man is a false minister with a work built upon shifting sand, while the other is a true minister with a work built on solid rock. The house built on the sand will fall; the house built on the rock will stand. So we see the most crucial factor is not *what* the wise and foolish men and the true and false ministers build, but *how and where* they build. Let me explain.

Every city has a building code that sets forth certain specifications by which every structure must be erected. And every building code specifies that the foundation of a house must be laid on firm, undisturbed soil or solid rock.

When I moved my family from Pennsylvania to the Atlantic coast of southern Florida years ago, I was startled to find that there was practically no soil there, only sand. Yet I was amazed to see many high-rise condominiums being. erected along the beaches. How could they build such tall buildings on sand, I wondered.

Then one day I watched workmen deep in a sandy excavation erect a tall, strange-looking machine called a piledriver and with it they began to pound many long vertical shafts of solid concrete deeply into the sand. Then I learned that beneath the sand, which covered our part of the state, lay a solid bed of rock coral. The concrete shafts were being driven down into that coral, creating the basis for a foundation that could support a structure many stories high. The Florida building code demanded just such a foundation.

To apply that illustration to our parable, we could say the wise man built his house by driving a foundation deep into the bedrock of dependence on the Word of God, while the foolish man built his house on the sand of doing his own thing. While outwardly the works were identical, the wise man built in *obedience* to the master building code, living a decent, moral life to the glory of God, while the foolish man built in disobedience to the master building code, indulging in selfishness and immorality. The wise man recognized and submitted to the authority over him, while the foolish man rebelled against that same authority.

But as the force and power of God's full revelation broke in upon the houses, the fatal mistake of the foolish man was revealed and the inevitable crash came. No structure built on a sandy foundation can stand for long.

I'm sure you see the parallel by now. The true minister of God wisely builds his ministry in submission to the Word of God—

the building code of Jesus, the Master Builder ("everyone who hears these words of mine and puts them into practice"), while the false minister foolishly builds his ministry—even though the signs and wonders that accompany it are genuine—in foolish rebellion against the Word of God ("every man who hears these words of mine and does not put them into practice"). The ministry of the true minister will be blessed and will stand firm through the flood of the final revelation of God's Spirit while the rebellious ministry of the false minister will surely collapse under the same revelation, its rebellious foundation finally exposed. When that happens, many precious people of God suffer severe spiritual injury.

It should sober us all to realize the number of powerful, nationally known ministries that have collapsed and disappeared in the past few years, their founders dead or disgraced, or out of ministry and lost to the present purposes of God. It should sober us even more to realize that there are current ministries of prominence whose moral foundations—from a scriptural standpoint—are questionable. The more God's power floods into such a ministry, the more likely the minister's rebellion and deception are to surface, the more rapid will be the erosion of that ministry's foundation, and the more imminent the collapse of the ministry.

We live in a strange and awesome time when God seems to be shaking everything that can be shaken in order that only those things that cannot be shaken will remain. (See Hebrews 12:27.) Therefore, let us not be misled or carried away by the flurry of signs and wonders that seem to abound even in the midst of questionable ministries. Let us not be swayed or taken in by the cries of the gullible who say, "But God is blessing the ministry with miracles!" for God often bestows His blessings on the unworthy as well as the worthy. "He causes his sun to rise on the evil and the good, and sends rain on the righteous and the unrighteous" (Matthew 5:45).

In the end, only those ministries based on the bedrock of obedience to the Word of God will stand.

10

God Can Restore the False Minister

For nine chapters we have been wrestling with the disturbing subject of false apostles, prophets, teachers, and elders. We discussed how serious the problem is today and how serious it was in the New Testament church. We've attempted to show how good men with good ministries fall prey to Satan and what the church and the ministers themselves can do to help prevent and control the problem.

But what about the fallen minister himself? Is there any real hope for him? For some, perhaps not. Some men seem to have passed the point of restoration. Peter speaks of their fate.

> If they have escaped the corruption of the world by knowing our Lord and Savior Jesus Christ and are again entangled in it and overcome, they are worse off at the end than they were at the beginning. It would have been better for them not to have known the way of righteousness, than to have known it and then to turn their backs on the sacred command that was passed on to them.
>
> 2 Peter 2:20–21

But for others who truly repent and earnestly seek restoration, God is faithful both to forgive and restore. For some, confession and repentance seem sufficient. For others, the Satanic bondage in their lives is so severe that in addition to confession and repentance, God must do a supernatural work to deliver them from demonic power. I want to share the story of one such dramatic deliverance that shows how even the worst false prophet can be redeemed, provided he will humble himself, confess his sin, and ask for deliverance and restoration.

The Reverend Gerald Elkins* was outwardly an effective servant of the Lord, recognized as one of the spiritual leaders in the large city where he pastored. Married to a lovely woman, he and his wife had reared three sons, all of whom were actively serving Christ. As one of the sponsoring ministers of the seminar where I was a speaker, he carried out his responsibilities with smooth efficiency. Then, in one session, I spoke on the subject of true and false prophets, knowing nothing of Elkins' personal problems. I did notice his face seemed unusually grave as he listened to the message.

The next evening, after the final session of the seminar, Elkins and his wife, accompanied by a minister friend, came to the home where my wife and I had been staying. Their minister friend had called earlier, saying the Elkinses had requested marital counseling.

Having been a church pastor and Bible teacher for many years, I have listened to many stories of deception and immorality among Christians and supposed I had just about heard it all. But the confession of Gerald Elkins that night surpassed them all. His proved to be the classic tale of a false minister; an effective spiritual leader whose personal life had become a hellish nightmare.

Reared by parents who were deeply involved in witchcraft and immorality, Elkins had suffered both sexual and spiritual abuse as a child. As a Christian minister he had been outwardly conscientious, devoted, and God-fearing, but secretly driven by unclean spirits, which controlled him. He had engaged in one sordid act of

---

* Not his real name.

adultery after another over the years until his personal life had deteriorated to the point where exposure seemed inevitable. His torment had become so acute, he told me, that immediately after each sexual encounter, he was not only filled with self-loathing, but feelings of rage and murder would rise within him. Only by exercising the strongest effort had he been able to refrain from killing his victims. The situation had become so hopeless he was seriously contemplating suicide. While aware her husband was under some terrible emotional strain, his wife either had no knowledge or would not let herself believe the nature and severity of his problem.

Because of the continuing emotional strain on their marriage, both Elkins and his wife had sought psychiatric help and even hospitalization, but with no significant relief. The whole destructive process had finally become so terrifying to him that Elkins could keep silent about his torment no longer. After listening to my message and just a few hours before our appointment, he confessed his whole sordid story, first to his minister friend, then to his wife.

"I have never been able to understand the contradiction in my own life," Elkins confessed to me. "I knew that when I ministered there was a real anointing from God. The gifts of the Holy Spirit would operate and lives would be blessed and changed by the power of God. Yet only hours later I would be involved in immorality again! Then I heard your teaching yesterday and recognized for the first time that I was a false prophet!"

Yet in spite of the years of immorality and deception, Gerald Elkins longed to be set free. Thank God, He knows our hearts! And He wants to redeem the false or fallen minister. Even though He must judge the deception and the sin, He longs to redeem those who are trapped in them.

So it proved in Gerald Elkins' case. Following a time of complete confession and deep repentance, Elkins prayed a profound, heart-wrenching prayer that God would forgive him, save his marriage, and somehow restore and redeem the lives of those he had seduced.

After his confession and prayer, he felt an overwhelming desire for deliverance from the evil spirits, which seemed to drive him to the shameful acts he had committed for so many years, and so he asked me to pray for him.

"I'm quite ready to pray," I said. "However, you must also accept responsibility for your actions and not blame it all on the devil. I have ministered to many people who have been similarly tormented, but who never gave up resisting; people who—despite their inner torments—refrained from actually committing the evil acts themselves."

"I know, I know!" he sobbed. "And I don't know what I can do to ever make it up to those poor women, but if God will give me another chance I will serve Him the rest of my life with purity and integrity." I agreed that only God could give him the grace to live a life that could atone for the tragedies of the past.

As we ministered to him, Elkins seemed to receive only a slight measure of help. There was some relief when a spirit of rejection left, sobbing and wailing. Although I was by no means satisfied with the results at that point, since it was already past midnight, he and his wife prepared to leave.

But God was not through with Gerald Elkins! As we joined hands for a closing prayer, I found myself coming against the influence of spiritualism and witchcraft, which Elkins earlier testified had plagued his family for generations. The Holy Spirit revealed that this influence was like a curse on Elkins' family and directed us to cancel that curse in the name of Jesus. As I spoke the words of that prayer, out of the corner of my eye I saw Gerald Elkins duck his head and hunch his shoulders.

I was holding his right hand and suddenly his grip became like a vise.

Glancing at his face I saw his eyes take on a glazed expression as a low, moaning growl began to spill from his lips and a strange white foam began to bubble out of his mouth.

"No! No! No!" The demonic protest bellowed out from somewhere deep within his body. Suddenly, some unseen force hurled Elkins headlong to the floor where he began to thrash wildly.

The other minister and I knelt beside him and—grabbing his shoulders—attempted to restrain the wild thrashing. Speaking above the growling sounds coming from his throat I urged him to take sides with God against the devil's torment and to renounce the spirit of witchcraft. Only after great strain and physical effort was he able to gasp out, "In the name of Jesus, I renounce witchcraft!"

Then, when we commanded the spirit of witchcraft to leave, Elkins became more violent than ever. The ensuing struggle lasted a full fifteen minutes until finally, with a long, gasping shriek, the demon left. Immediately, Elkins went limp as a rag on the floor.

Then I saw a strange and beautiful thing. Spread-eagled and face down, he began patting the floor gently with one hand, and softly began to praise God. "Oh, thank You Jesus!" he exclaimed. "Thank You for Your love and mercy! Thank You for setting me free!"

Only Elkins was not yet free. The deliverance process resumed with demon after demon surfacing in his personality, screaming with rage, attempting to choke him, and throwing him bodily around the room. There were demons of lust, adultery, perversion, hatred, and murder, which named themselves and were cast out. The demon of murder screamed and boasted, "I'll kill him before I come out! He's mine! I'll never leave him; I'll kill him first!" It came out raging and protesting to the last.

Then, the most amazing thing of all happened, something that brought me into a deeper appreciation of the compassion of God than I ever had before. Weak and exhausted as he was, Elkins propped himself up on one elbow and smiled at me through tears of relief.

"I know now, the promise was real!" he exclaimed.

I was puzzled. "What promise?"

"The promise God gave me from the Scriptures yesterday," Elkins replied. "He gave it to me even before I had confessed all those horrible things to my wife, when I was still in the midst of all that degradation, still filled with shame and horror over the way I had been living, when I didn't know whether either my marriage or my life would be spared. Right then, God promised He would deliver me!"

I still didn't know what he was talking about.

"I was sitting in my living room at home, contemplating suicide," Elkins continued. "Then I reached for the newspaper to try to get my mind off the horror I was experiencing. But there was a book on top of the newspaper; it was my wife's Bible. When I picked it up, it just fell open and I began to read. I'd never seen the passage before, but it spoke so clearly to my situation that tears came to my eyes. What it said seemed too good to be true. I didn't believe God could love anyone that much—especially not me, not after the kind of life I'd led. But it is true; He does love me and He's setting me free!"

Then Gerald Elkins slumped to the floor once more and began weeping for joy once again. "Oh, the peace!" he cried. "The peace that comes when Jesus sets you free!"

I sat with the others, watching Elkins, curiosity about the Scripture growing in my mind. Before I could say anything, he sat up once more and turned to his wife.

"Honey, would you go out to the car and get your Bible? I want to show them the passage." He turned to me. "It's in *The Living Bible* translation," he explained.

His wife returned with her Bible and handed it to Elkins who passed it on to me. "Read Isaiah 33, verses 17 through 24," he said.

I found the place and began to read aloud:

> Your eyes will see the King in his beauty, and the highlands
> of heaven far away. Your mind will think back to this time
> of terror—

And that's as far as I got. At the word *terror* Elkins screamed in agony and hit the floor once more. Like some giant misshapen crab he began to scuttle away from us.

"I'm afraid!" the demon speaking through him screamed. "Don't read those holy words! They make me afraid!" Then—with no help at all from us—Elkins recovered control of himself, renounced the spirit of terror, and it left with a long, choking wail. Instantly, Elkins was calm again.

"Thank You, Jesus!" he exclaimed, sitting up once more. "That demon couldn't stand hearing the Word of God promising my deliverance. Read the rest of it! Go on, read it!" And tears of joy filled his eyes once more.

And in one of the most profoundly moving experiences of my life, I read the precious promise God gave Gerald Elkins, before He delivered him.

> Your eyes will see the King in his beauty and the highlands of heaven far away. Your mind will think back to this time of terror when the Assyrian officers outside your walls—

"They represent the demons that controlled and tormented me," Elkins interrupted.

> —are counting your towers and estimating how much they will get from your fallen city. *But soon they will all be gone. These fierce, violent people, with a strange, jabbering language you can't understand, will disappear.*
>
> Instead, you will see Jerusalem at peace, a place where God is worshiped, a city quiet and unmoved. The glorious Lord will be to us as a wide river of protection, and no enemy can cross. For the Lord is our Judge, our Lawgiver, and our King; he will care for us and save us. The enemies' sails hang loose on broken masts with useless tackle. Their treasure will be divided by the people of God; even the lame will win their share. The people of Israel will no longer say, "We are sick and helpless," for the Lord will forgive them their sins and bless them.
>
> Isaiah 33:17–24, LB, italics added

I could not restrain my own tears as I read. I saw how the Lord knew the exact moment that Gerald Elkins could receive his deliverance. At the very moment the devil and his demons were boasting of their complete capture of that beaten, tormented man of God, God supernaturally intervened to set him free.

Both Gerald Elkins and I knew that the future would hold severe times of testing as he purposed to walk in the light of the marvelous grace God had extended to him. And the few times I have been in touch with him in the years since, he tells me maintaining his victory has not been easy, yet he continues to walk out his promise to God in faith.

In Gerald Elkins' dramatic deliverance I saw the determination of God to bring forth a ministry in the body of Christ that is pure as well as powerful. He stands ready to forgive and restore every false or fallen minister who will repent and submit to the care and assistance of faithful brothers and sisters who stand ready to come to his aid.

Yet as terrible as the problem of dishonest and immoral ministers is, as successful as the devil has been in trapping devoted servants of God in all kinds of perverse sin, and as faithful as God is to save and restore those who repent and seek His help, there is yet an even more subtle—perhaps even more deadly—form of spiritual warfare going on in the body of Christ. It is a warfare in which Satan has successfully involved practically every believer, either as an aggressor or as a victim. I call it *the deadliest war of all*. We will examine that war next.

11

The Deadliest War of All

Some time ago I received a letter from a lady in Phoenix, Arizona. After thanking me for something she'd read in one of my books, she added:

> "We are sorry to hear that Rev. David King* has become an alcoholic. His ministry has been a blessing to thousands. All the members of our church are praying he will repent and be delivered from his terrible affliction."

I was shocked and angered by her letter. Shocked because the man she was referring to was a personal friend; angered because I knew what she had heard about him was untrue. I called her on the telephone.

"Where did you hear such a vicious rumor?" I asked. Relieved to learn that what she had heard was not true, she said, "A local minister told the women in our prayer group. He claimed he had

---

* Not his real name.

proof." And she gave me the minister's name and address. I immediately sent him a letter.

> *Dear Rev_____:*
> It has come to my attention that you have sought to destroy the reputation of a friend of mine, the Rev. David King, by publicly accusing him of being an alcoholic. Such a serious charge demands verification. Therefore, within the next ten days I intend to fly to your city, accompanied by two colleagues, to hear your accusation personally, and to examine any proof you may have in support of it. Please call my office and confirm a time when we can meet.

I sent the letter by registered mail. Three mornings later my telephone rang. It was my friend's accuser and there was something akin to panic in his voice.

"Mr. Basham, I just received your letter and I'm calling to apologize for what I said and to beg you to cancel your trip. I don't know what made me say those things about David King. I suppose I was just jealous of his ministry. I know he is a man of God, but I heard someone say he drank and I guess I got carried away when I repeated the rumor. Please forgive me! I have already sent a letter to David King apologizing for lying about him and asking his forgiveness, so there is no need for you to fly out here."

I agreed to cancel my trip, but pointed out how impossible it would be to repair all the damage caused by his evil accusation. Slander, once made public, can never be totally refuted. Like birds let out of a cage, such words defy recapture and fly wildly in all directions. Before our conversation ended, the chastened pastor apologized once more, fervently promising to guard his tongue in the future.

The incident I have just described was only one small, nasty battle in what I have come to call *the deadliest war of all.* But for every battle we win in that war (if it is even correct to say that particular battle was won!) there are a thousand more the devil wins. In previous chapters we have considered the subject of immorality among Christians almost entirely from the standpoint of so-called "gross sin"—that is, sexual and financial immorality. But there is a far more vicious, far more pervasive, far more deadly form of immorality masquerading in our midst. *This "deadliest*

*war of all" is the socially acceptable but tragic practice of slander
and character assassination. It is the spiritual slaughter we
practice every time we open our mouths to criticize, malign,
accuse, or condemn another believer.* Moreover, when challenged
we usually try to justify the evil practice by describing it with
innocent-sounding phrases: "I was merely giving my opinion" or
"It just came up in casual conversation."

But describing this despicable activity as "stating our opinion"
or "casual conversation" is about as honest as calling adultery
"sleeping together" and abortion "removing fetal tissue." It is the
devil's way of referring to a terrible sin as a harmless occur-
rence—something on the order of Nazis in Germany in World
War II calling the Holocaust "dealing with the Jewish problem."
Nevertheless, libel and slander, like the raw chemical wastes that
poison the pure waters of our nation's lakes and rivers, have pol-
luted their way into every church, dishonoring commitments,
spawning suspicion, betraying trust, undermining personal integrity, and poisoning Christian relationships.

The Warfare in Scripture

We find Jesus predicting this deadly form of spiritual warfare
in Matthew 24, where He lists the conditions that will prevail at
the close of the age. First, He describes various physical upheavals
in the world and then He pictures the persecution Christians can
expect from unbelievers.

> Then they will hand you over to suffer affliction and tribula-
> tion, and put you to death; and you will be hated by all na-
> tions for My name's sake.
>
> Matthew 24:9, AMPLIFIED

But Jesus' prediction of persecution does not end with what "the
nations" will do to Christians; He goes on to describe the
church's own tragic civil war.

> And then many will be offended and repelled and begin to
> distrust and desert [Him Whom they ought to trust and
> obey] and will stumble and fall away, *and betray one another*

and pursue one another with hatred . . . and the love [agape]
of the great body of people will grow cold, because of the
multiplied lawlessness and iniquity.
                    Matthew 24:10–12, AMPLIFIED, italics added

The word for "lawlessness" is the Greek word *anomos*,
which stands not only for wicked or evil deeds, but literally means
"contempt for or violation of the law." Lawlessness means "lack
of accountability" and it is this very lack of accountability that
contributes so powerfully to the deadliest war of all.

A minister I know was being repeatedly slandered and libeled
by another clergyman in the same city. His attacker had become
so bitterly offended that he had even published a libelous book
condemning the ministry of the man he disliked. Following the
instructions in Matthew 18:15—"If your brother sins against you,
go and show him his fault, just between the two of you" —my
friend finally called at his critic's office to confront him. Although
obviously embarrassed, the minister flatly refused to accept accountability for his slander and libel.

"You're taking this whole thing much too seriously," he blus-
tered, and refused to discuss it further, as if the whole matter was
insignificant. But no deliberate attempt at character assassination
can be called insignificant!

The Scriptures contain many serious warnings against slander,
beginning with the ninth commandment. "You shall not give
false testimony against your neighbor" (Exodus 20:16). Ironically,
that verse appears immediately following three commandments
that state, respectively: you shall not murder; you shall not commit adultery; and you shall not steal. But while almost every
Christian claims to abhor murder, adultery, and theft and strives
to obey the commands against those sins, somehow slander or
giving false testimony is embraced as something less than sin. In
fact, we engage in it with relish and self-righteous zeal, accepting
no accountability and feeling no guilt or remorse for our words.
Perhaps no other command in all Scripture suffers such near total
disregard. Yet there are many additional verses that not only condemn slander but gravely warn of the judgment awaiting those
who engage in it. Here are a few:

"I am the Lord your God. Do not steal. Do not lie. Do not deceive one another . . . Do not go about spreading slander among your people."

Leviticus 19:10–11, 16

If a malicious witness takes the stand to accuse a man . . . and if the witness proves to be a liar, giving false testimony against his brother, then do to him as he intended to do to his brother. You must purge the evil from among you.

Deuteronomy 19:16–19

Whoever slanders his neighbor in secret, him will I put to silence . . . no one who speaks falsely will stand in my presence.

Psalm 101:5, 7

A false witness will not go unpunished, and he who pours out lies will not go free.

Proverbs 19:5

"Do not judge, or you too will be judged. For in the same way you judge others, you will be judged, and with the measure you use, it will be measured to you. Why do you look at the speck of sawdust in your brother's eye and pay no attention to the plank in your own eye? . . . You hypocrite, first take the plank out of your own eye, and then you will see clearly to remove the speck from your brother's eye."

Matthew 7:1–3, 5

"But I tell you that men will have to give account on the day of judgment for every careless word they have spoken. For by your words you will be acquitted, and by your words you will be condemned."

Matthew 12:36–37

You, then, why do you judge your brother? Or why do you look down on your brother? For we will all stand before God's judgment seat. . . . So then, each of us will give an account of himself to God. Therefore let us stop passing judgment on one another.

Romans 14:10, 12–13

Brothers, do not slander one another. Anyone who speaks against his brother or judges him speaks against the law . . . who are you to judge your neighbor?

James 4:11–12

It Can Happen To You

I first felt the shock of being deliberately lied about by fellow Christians while in Bible college in Oklahoma more than thirty years ago. My wife and I had begun a weekly prayer meeting in our home near the campus. There were miracles of healing and a number of student ministers and their wives received the baptism in the Holy Spirit with the scriptural evidence of speaking in tongues.

But the denomination to which I belonged held the position that miracles could not happen today, so reaction to the vital spiritual activity in our meetings was not long in coming. Gossip, accusations, and vicious rumors swept over the campus like wildfire. Alice and I were at first shocked, then stunned, then angered, and finally deeply saddened by the lies spread by our Christian classmates. They claimed we were holding seances and practicing witchcraft. We were accused of hypnotizing one another and falling into trances. It was widely reported that we turned out the lights to conduct wild sex orgies and engage in wife swapping. Some students even attempted to circulate a petition to have us expelled from the university.

The slander didn't stop with the students. In class one day, a professor whom I had considered a personal friend was asked his opinion of "the group on campus that believes in speaking in tongues." He smiled over my head and replied, "They are just unstable young Christians who work themselves up into an emotional frenzy and then begin jabbering at one another like monkeys." Unable or unwilling to accept the validity of any spiritual experience beyond his own, he resorted to lying ridicule.

Almost twenty-five years later I received a respectful letter from a young seminary student who challenged this same professor (who by then was teaching in a California seminary) about his condemnation of the worldwide charismatic renewal in the church. In defense of the renewal the seminarian quoted from some books of nationally recognized ministries in the renewal, including my own. According to his letter, the professor resorted once more to slander. "Basham was a student of mine in Oklahoma years ago," he told his California class. "He and his friends fell into heresy and fanaticism. They ended up in sexual immorality and were almost expelled from seminary."

"Because of your widely recognized ministry today," the young man's letter to me graciously added, "I'm sure if such a thing did happen you have long since found forgiveness and restoration."

Saddened at the thought of all the years and all the times in all the classes in which that professor had continued to lie about me, I answered the seminarian's letter assuring him our group had been innocent victims of the devil's reviling. I also sent him and his classmates complimentary copies of my book *Face Up with a Miracle*, which contained my personal testimony, including an account of those powerful but painful days at Phillips University in Oklahoma.

In the years since that first encounter with persecution in seminary, there have been some additional storms of slander, libel, and persecution. I find a kind of bitter irony in the fact that it is precisely because there is so much immorality in the church today and because there are so many false ministers preying upon the people of God that the devil seems to have the best of both worlds. Not only does he succeed in fanning unholy fires of immorality among some believers, but is able at the same time to goad other gullible Christians into crucifying respectable ministries and innocent believers with vicious lies and slander!

Exposing the Accuser

One reason why we fall into the trap of maligning and slandering one another is that we are largely ignorant of or indifferent to the devil in his role as "the accuser." The very word *devil* literally means slanderer or accuser. Revelation 12:10 refers to the devil as "the accuser of our brothers, who accuses them before our God day and night." Note that his accusations are ceaseless. There is no end to his vicious campaign to discredit Christians in the eyes of God, in the eyes of each other, and even in their own eyes.

One morning some years ago I awoke and lay in bed quietly

praying. Ministry the night before had been fruitful; my family and I were healthy and prosperous and I was more than a little grateful to God. I was feeling so good that when the telephone rang, I almost answered it with, "Praise the Lord!" instead of "Hello." I was totally unprepared for the stream of vitriolic condemnation that spewed into my ear.

"Just who the _____ do you think you are, Don Basham," a snarly voice began. "You think you are some high and mighty, big shot Bible teacher, but let me tell you what you really are!" And there followed a barrage of vicious obscenities, accusations, and condemnations that lasted a full three minutes. Too surprised to interrupt at first, I finally realized the true source of the attack and shouted into the receiver, "Satan, I rebuke you in the name of Jesus!" There was instant silence, followed by the click of the receiver.

Stunned and shaken by the assault, I lay staring at the receiver still in my hand. Then the familiar words of Jesus from the Sermon on the Mount came to mind:

> "Blessed are you when people insult you, persecute you and falsely say all kinds of evil against you because of me. Rejoice and be glad, because great is your reward in heaven."
> Matthew 5:11–12

At that moment, Alice entered the bedroom announcing breakfast was ready. Then she asked, "Who was on the telephone, dear?" I gently replaced the receiver. "I guess we'll never know," I replied. "But I believe a small sum may just have been deposited in our heavenly bank account."

The ceaseless activity of "the accuser" is clear evidence of his determination to destroy the church by goading its members into defaming each other by lies and slander. It's a problem as old as the church itself. As Paul warns the Galatians, "If you keep on biting and devouring each other, watch out or you will be destroyed by each other" (Galatians 5:15).

But thankfully, the Scriptures also remind us that we have a Divine Advocate who continually intercedes for us in this vicious and deadly war. Hebrews 7:25–26 speaks of Jesus our High Priest, holy, blameless, set apart from sinners, exalted above the heavens who "always lives to intercede" for us.

So a cosmic scene stands in clear focus. Satan with his unceasing slander of us before God and his tireless campaign to goad us into slandering each other, being steadily withstood by Jesus Christ, our Savior and Great High Priest who sits at the right hand of God, who "always lives to intercede" for us, praying to the Father in our behalf for the eventual fulfillment of His own prayer "that all of them be one" (John 17:21).

Since lies make up such a significant portion of Satan's weaponry, let's take some time to examine what the Bible has to say about some of the different kinds of lies we encounter and their effect on us.

12

Bearing False Witness

Both from the Word of God and our own experiences we know there are many reasons for lying. We lie to protect ourselves and our reputations; we lie to justify our actions; we lie to avoid criticism or escape punishment; we lie out of spite and envy; we lie out of hate and rage; we lie to promote ourselves at the expense of others; we lie to hurt those who have hurt us. Sometimes it seems we lie just for the sake of lying.

But when we examine Scripture we discover God does not judge all falsehood with equal severity. All lying is sinful, but some lies seem almost inconsequential while others are treacherous and deadly. Since God alone knows our hearts, He alone has the right to judge the gravity of any lie we may utter. For this very reason the Lord sternly warns us not to judge each other. (See Matthew 7:1–5.)

Here are four categories and examples of lying taken from Scripture with comments on the motives that seemed to provoke the lies. We begin with the less significant falsehoods and end with the deadlier ones.

Lying Out of Fear

Genesis 18:9–15 Sarah lies about laughing

When the Lord told Abraham that his wife Sarah would bear a son, Sarah, who was listening outside the tent, laughed at the thought. But when confronted by the angel of God, she denied she had laughed.

> Then the Lord said to Abraham, "Why did Sarah laugh and say, 'Will I really have a child now that I am old?' " . . . Sarah was afraid so she lied and said, "I did not laugh." But he said, "Yes, you did laugh."
>
> Genesis 18:13, 15

So Sarah lied, but once she was confronted with the lie, that was the end of the matter. There seem to have been no further consequences to her act.

Genesis 12:10–20 Abraham asks Sarah to lie and say she is his sister

In this story a fearful Abraham persuades his wife to lie to Pharaoh's soldiers to keep them from killing him. Once again, fear is the motive. While the Scripture records no correction of Abraham or Sarah by God on this occasion, the Bible records other examples of more serious lying.

Matthew 26:69–75 Peter lies about knowing Jesus

After Jesus was arrested in the Garden of Gethsemane and the other disciples had scattered out of fear, Peter followed Jesus and the soldiers into the courtyard of the high priest. When he was recognized as one of Jesus' disciples, Peter lied three times, cursed, and swore he had never known Jesus, even as Jesus had prophesied: "Peter, before the rooster crows today, you will deny three times that you know me" (Luke 22:34).

Peter's only punishment for lying was the remorse he felt—

"and he went outside and wept bitterly" (Matthew 26:75)—a remorse he had to endure until he made peace with Jesus again, after the resurrection. (See John 21:15–19.)

Lying Out of Spite

Genesis 39 records the story of Joseph as a slave in Potiphar's house. Scripture says that from the time Potiphar placed Joseph in charge of his household "the blessing of the Lord was on everything Potiphar had" (verse 5). Everything, apparently, except Potiphar's lustful young wife. When she tried to seduce Joseph and failed, out of spite she lied to her servants and her husband, claiming Joseph had tried to force himself on her. Although totally innocent, Joseph was thrown into prison. The whole incident seems terribly unfair until we realize that it is just one more dramatic step in Joseph's divine destiny, a destiny that led him to become ruler of Egypt and a savior of his own people.

Lying To Cover Disobedience Or Escape Punishment

This third category of lying is more serious than the first since lying to cover disobedience or to escape punishment generally involves shifting the blame for our own sin to someone else.

Genesis 3:1–12 Adam and Eve and the forbidden fruit

The earliest scriptural example of lying to cover disobedience or escape punishment is found in this passage where God confronts Adam for eating the forbidden fruit.

> "Have you eaten from the tree that I commanded you not to eat from?"
>
> Genesis 3:11

With those words God gives Adam clear opportunity to repent and make a simple confession that he had sinned. Who knows how man's destiny might have been altered had Adam confessed and repented! But, of course, he didn't. Rather he shifted blame for his own disobedience to his wife.

"The woman you put here with me—she gave me some
fruit from the tree, and I ate it."

Genesis 3:12

Adam didn't deny he ate the fruit, but by shifting the blame to
Eve he lied in denying responsibility for his own sin. In fact, in
his sullen determination to escape accountability—a sin that
seems to dominate the "deadliest war of all"—he blames both
God and Eve. "It's all your fault, God! Yours and that woman
You gave me! I never even touched that tree! She's the one who
actually took the fruit; I just took a bite from her!" While Eve
was not guiltless, God had entrusted to Adam the responsibility
for watching over his wife, therefore He held Adam responsible
for the sin. (See Gen.3:17–19.)

The awesome, terrible result of Adam's and Eve's disobedience
and Adam's lying about his part in the sin was their expulsion
from the Garden of Eden and the fall of mankind.

Exodus 32:1–35 Aaron and the golden calf

While Moses was on Mount Sinai receiving the Ten Commandments, the Israelites rebelled against Jehovah and persuaded
Aaron to fashion a golden calf for them to worship. Aaron not
only took the lead in making the golden calf, he even built an
altar so the Israelites could offer pagan sacrifices (Exodus 32:2–5).

But when Moses returned to destroy the golden calf and de-
mand an explanation from Aaron, Aaron shifted the blame to the
Israelites and lied about his own involvement in the rebellion.
Once more we witness the attempt to escape accountability.

"Do not be angry, my lord. . . . You know how prone these
people are to evil. They said to me, 'Make us gods' . . . Then
they gave me the gold and *I threw it into the fire and out
came this calf!*"

Exodus 32:22–24, italics added

Were the sin of Aaron not so grievous, we could laugh at his
ludicrous lie that the golden calf miraculously appeared out of the

fire. Perhaps Aaron thought his explanation would be more believable if he included a miracle in his lie!

But Scripture makes it plain that Aaron was responsible for what happened to the Israelites while Moses was on Mount Sinai.

> Moses saw that the people were running wild and that *Aaron had let them get out of control,* and so become a laughingstock to their enemies.
>
> Exodus 32:25, italics added

Because of the rebellion, 3000 Israelites were slaughtered and God promised even further punishment.

Samuel 10:1-8; 13:1-14 Saul lies to Samuel

In the life of King Saul we find a third example of lying to cover disobedience and escape punishment. When Samuel anointed Saul king over Israel, he listed certain signs that would be fulfilled and then instructed Saul in a certain course of action.

> "Once these signs are fulfilled, do whatever your hand finds to do, for God is with you. Go down ahead of me to Gilgal. I will surely come down to you to sacrifice burnt offerings and fellowship offerings, but you must wait seven days until I come to you and tell you what you are to do."
>
> 1 Samuel 10:7-8

But in chapter 13 we read how Saul failed to wait for Samuel's arrival in Gilgal. He arrogantly usurped the rights of the priesthood to offer a burnt offering in Samuel's absence. In lying to justify his disobedience, Saul first blamed his men: "When I saw the men were scattering"; then he blamed Samuel: "and when you did not come at the set time"; and finally he excused himself: "*I felt compelled* to offer the burnt offering" (1 Samuel 13:11-12, italics added).

But Saul lies to no avail. His disobedience is so grievous in God's sight that from that very moment Saul's days as king are numbered. (See 1 Samuel 13:13-14).

Plotting or Lying Out of Evil Ambition

When we examine lies in Scripture that are motivated by evil ambition or conspiracy, we uncover sin God considers an abomination. Lies borne out of simple fear or even out of a desire to escape punishment are far less serious than conspiratorial lying. Perhaps more than any other activity, conspiracy reveals the evil intent in a man's heart. Lying borne of fear reveals weakness, but lying borne of conspiracy reveals wickedness. And as we noted earlier, there is a vast difference between weakness and wickedness.

Conspiracy involves wicked plotting and scheming. It involves premeditation. Even in our own system of justice, premeditated crime is punished far more severely than unpremeditated crime. When one man kills another and the killing is unpremeditated, the crime is called manslaughter and the punishment may be relatively light—one to three years in prison or perhaps even a suspended sentence. However, if the killing is planned or premeditated, if lying in wait was involved, then the punishment may be life imprisonment or even death by execution.

According to the Mosaic law, if a man accidentally kills another man, he could escape vengeance or punishment by fleeing to a city of refuge provided specifically as a sanctuary for such situations. (See Deuteronomy 19:1–7.) But the law also stated that any man guilty of *premeditated* murder was not entitled to such protection but would forfeit his own life for his evil deed. (See Deuteronomy 19:11–13). Now let us look at some biblical examples of premeditated or conspiratorial lying.

2 Samuel 15:1–12 Absalom's conspiracy against David

Absalom, King David's third son, conspired to steal the loyalty of David's subjects by a campaign of lying about his father. The conspiracy proved so successful that David and his officers were forced to leave Jerusalem and flee for their lives. While David's fatherly concern for the welfare of the evil son bent on killing him and stealing his throne is touching (see 2 Samuel 18:5), Absalom's conspiracy is so wicked in the eyes of God that it marked him out for death.

> For the Lord had determined . . . to bring disaster on Absalom.
>
> 2 Samuel 17:14

The conspiracy ends in failure and despite David's fatherly pleas that his son be spared, Absalom is slain.

Acts 5:1–10 The conspiracy of Ananias and Sapphira

The story we are now about to examine is one of the most sobering in all Scripture. It records God's swift and awesome judgment against a conspiratorial lie. At first reading, God's judgment against these two prominent members of the early church may seem unnecessarily severe. But we must remember that the incident took place in the days immediately following Pentecost, when life in the church was at the peak of its purity and power.

> All the believers were one in heart and mind. No one claimed that any of his possessions was his own, but they shared everything they had. With great power the apostles continued to testify to the resurrection of the Lord Jesus, and much grace was upon them all.
>
> Acts 4:32–33

As an expression of their deep commitment, some believers sold houses and lands and brought the money to the apostles for them to distribute. Acts 5:1–10 records how Ananias and Sapphira also sold a piece of property, but then—in their own little private conspiracy—plotted to keep a part of the price for themselves while giving the rest to the apostles, *as if they were giving it all.* In other words, they *conspired* to gain a better reputation than they deserved.

But when Ananias presented the money to the apostles as if it were truly a sacrificial gift, by revelation Peter declared that he and his wife had lied to the Holy Spirit. Ananias dropped dead!

Later, when his wife Sapphira came in, Peter carefully offered her the opportunity to admit the conspiracy. Instead, Sapphira repeated the lie of her husband. When Peter revealed that their conspiracy was known, she also fell dead at his feet. With such awesome and immediate judgment against their conspiracy, it is little wonder that "great fear seized the whole church and all who heard about these events" (Acts 5:11).

Let us note again that by contemporary standards, the swift judgment against Ananias and Sapphira seems terribly severe. Perhaps it was because of the pure and holy status of the infant church in those early, miracle-filled days that the sin of Ananias and Sapphira, by contrast, seemed so wicked.

But there was also the deliberate, conspiratorial nature of their sin. Ananias and Sapphira *plotted* to defraud the Holy Spirit. They conspired to achieve a holy reputation by means of an unholy deception. On the strength of a shameful lie, they sought equal status with selfless saints who gave everything. Such wicked scheming opened both of them to Satanic control. In fact, in their evil attempt to secure for themselves a higher standing than they deserved in that noble assembly, we see intimations of Lucifer's (Satan's) own initial perverted ambition:

> "I will raise my throne.... I will sit enthroned on the mount of assembly.... I will ascend.... I will make myself like the Most High."
>
> Isaiah 14:13–14

So, it was not just the lie, it was the conspiracy behind the lie that made their act so abominable. Wickedness is more than just ordinary wrong-doing; it is deliberate, premeditated evil. And it is the wicked element of premeditation that lies at the heart of the kind of lie we will discuss next: that deadliest lie of all—blasphemy against the Holy Spirit.

13

Blasphemy Against the Holy Spirit: A Sober Warning

The sin of blasphemy against the Holy Spirit falls in a category all to itself. It is obviously the most dangerous and deadly of all lies for it is called "the unpardonable sin." Therefore, we need a careful and accurate definition of it, not only to help relieve the fears of those Christians who mistakenly believe they may have committed it, but also to sound a sober warning about the dangerous position we may place ourselves in when we bear false witness, or when we deliberately criticize and condemn each other.

In over thirty years of ministry I have counseled and prayed with many Christians who mistakenly believed they were guilty of the unforgivable sin; that they had blasphemed the Holy Spirit. Some of them I was able to help, others I was not. Among the sins they confessed to me were lying, stealing, adultery, homosexuality, abortion, cursing God, abusing or abandoning children, forsaking the ministry, plus many other selfish, stupid things Christians do when they sin. But scripturally, none of those things qualifies as blasphemy against the Holy Spirit, the one unforgivable sin.

The word for blasphemy, in its various forms, appears in the

Bible a total of fifty-nine times. According to *The New Bible Dictionary,* blasphemy is "an act of affrontery in which the honor of God is insulted by man."[1] A simpler definition states that blasphemy is "cursing God." In Leviticus 24, God commands that a man be stoned to death because he "blasphemed the name of the Lord with a curse" (verse 11). In 1 Kings 21, Jezebel plotted to steal Naboth's vineyard for her husband, King Ahab, by persuading two evil men to testify that the innocent Naboth "did blaspheme God," thus assuring he would be stoned to death (verses 9–15).

In the New Testament, the Jews falsely accused Jesus of blasphemy on at least three occasions: first, when He forgave the sins of the paralytic (Mark 2:6–7), second, when they said He claimed to be God (John 10:33), and third, when, before the high priest, He finally confessed that He was the Christ (Matthew 26:62–64).

In Acts 26, Paul admitted in his defense before King Agrippa that before his conversion he had tried to force Christians to blaspheme—that is, curse the Lord Jesus (verse 11), and later confessed to Timothy that he himself was a "blasphemer" to whom God had shown mercy (1 Timothy 1:13).

But blasphemy itself—even though it means "cursing God"—does not preclude forgiveness, as Paul gratefully discovered. Nevertheless, one particular blasphemy, blasphemy against the Holy Spirit, still stands as the unforgivable sin. Where do we find it in Scripture and how does it differ from other forms of blasphemy? *It is crucial that we see the scriptural context in which blasphemy against the Holy Spirit is identified, since that context alone can determine its exact definition.*

Let me warn you, however, that the analysis that follows may make you uncomfortable, even a little fearful. I confess it affected me that way. Studying the scriptural material on this subject and the conclusions they led me to sobered me mightily. I came to the conclusion that most of us modern Christians gravely underestimate how serious slander is in the eyes of God, especially slander against Christians who minister in the supernatural power of the

---

[1] The New Bible Dictionary, InterVarsity Press, Leicester, Eng., 1962, p. 159.

Holy Spirit. God considers it more than weakness; He considers it wickedness. We are so conditioned to seeing and hearing only the pleasant and encouraging things about God and His dealings with us, that we find it quite difficult to examine a form of sin that clearly arouses His wrath. It makes us feel uneasy and vulnerable. But however inadequate it may be, I pray this brief look at the unpardonable sin will help create in all of us, not condemnation, but a holy fear of God—the kind the Psalmist spoke of when he said, "The fear of the Lord is clean, enduring forever" (Psalm 19:9, NAS).

Blasphemy against the Holy Spirit, apparently the one sin the blood of Christ does not atone for, is identified and denounced by Jesus Himself in Matthew 12. After He cast a deaf and dumb spirit out of a man, most of the crowd who witnessed the deliverance marveled, while the Pharisees condemned both Jesus and the miracle. But rather than accusing Him of mere blasphemy as they did previously, this time they laid the even more wicked charge that His ministry was inspired and controlled by Satan. They said, "It is only by Beelzebub, the prince of demons, that this fellow drives out demons" (Matthew 12:24). It is in response to this *specific* slander, this one particular lie *only*, that Jesus says:

> "I tell you, every sin and blasphemy will be forgiven men, but the blasphemy against the Spirit will not be forgiven. Anyone who speaks a word against the Son of Man will be forgiven, but anyone who speaks against the Holy Spirit will not be forgiven, either in this age or in the age to come."
>
> Matthew 12:31–32

Mark's account of the same incident says:

> "I tell you the truth, all the sins and blasphemies of men will be forgiven them. But whoever blasphemes against the Holy Spirit will never be forgiven; he is guilty of an eternal sin." He said this because they were saying, "He has an evil spirit."
>
> Mark 3:28–30

So then what is blasphemy against the Holy Spirit? The scriptural context seems to make it unmistakably clear: to blaspheme against the Holy Spirit is to deliberately proclaim the power of God to be the power of Satan. It is to define the Holy Spirit's power as demonic power; it is to "speak against the Holy Spirit" by deliberately accusing one anointed by the Holy Spirit of being under the control of Satan. We could even say that one who blasphemes against the Holy Spirit insinuates that God is Satan or Satan is God.

By their blasphemy, the Pharisees implied Jesus had switched his allegiance from God to Satan, even as the devil unsuccessfully tempted Him to during their confrontation in the wilderness. "So, if you worship me, [these kingdoms] will all be yours" (Luke 4:7). Now, through the lying mouths of the Pharisees, Satan is arrogantly boasting that Jesus has indeed betrayed the Father and has finally succumbed to that very temptation. Such blasphemy reaffirms Satan's ancient but thwarted ambition to dethrone God and take His place. (See Isaiah 14:12–15.)

Scripturally, then, no sin seems more grievous or more deadly than this particular slander, this deliberate "speaking against the Holy Spirit." Jesus would even pray the Father would forgive those who crucified Him, but in His stark and unrelenting denunciation of this sin, we see reflected a side of God's nature most Christians shudder even to contemplate; we see the awful wrath of an offended God. The writer of Hebrews describes a similar wrath against all those who have "insulted the Spirit of grace."

> If we deliberately keep on sinning after we have received the knowledge of the truth, no sacrifice for sins is left, but only a fearful expectation of judgment and of raging fire that will consume the enemies of God. Anyone who rejected the law of Moses died without mercy on the testimony of two or three witnesses. How much more severely do you think a man deserves to be punished who has trampled the Son of God under foot, who has treated as an unholy thing the blood of the covenant that sanctified him, and who has insulted the Spirit of grace? . . . It is a dreadful thing to fall into the hands of the living God.
>
> Hebrews 10:26–29, 31

Who Can Commit the Unpardonable Sin?

Now that we have defined blasphemy against the Holy Spirit, an even more urgent question follows: Who can commit this unpardonable sin?

Obviously, the Pharisees who first laid the terrible accusation against Jesus are guilty. But Jesus didn't limit His warning to the Pharisees. He said, "*Anyone* who speaks against the Holy Spirit will not be forgiven" (Matthew 12:32, italics added). The universal "anyone" includes others besides those in Jesus' immediate hearing. That, presumably, includes us, which means that His admonition about committing the sin of blasphemy against the Holy Spirit clearly warrants the same sober consideration we give to all the other admonitions of Scripture.

We also need to note that while superficially it may have seemed only another condemnation of Jesus' ministry by the Pharisees, had their sin been *only* against Jesus, He would have forgiven them, just as He forgave those who later crucified Him. But in this case, their blasphemy was clearly more than a condemnation of Him. Rather it was an offense against God in heaven who saw the slander as an unforgivable assault on the person and honor of the Holy Spirit.

Is there not a lesson here for us? Does it not say something to us about how grieved the Father is over our verbal judgments, our angry denunciation of other servants of God who live and minister by the power of the Holy Spirit and who—for all their differences—are as committed to the Lord as we are? Does it not also suggest that our condemnation of each other's testimonies, doctrines, and ministries may register with God as acts of wickedness far, far worse than other kinds of lying?

The seriousness with which God seems to view this kind of slander makes me agonize about those times I have been so quick to condemn a brother or sister in the Lord or to suggest their ministry or testimony may be spurious. Scripture makes it clear that the unpardonable sin is a sin committed with the tongue. Could I have said things about them that God might consider unforgivable?

Many ministers and Bible teachers maintain the only people

capable of blasphemy against the Holy Spirit are sinners who have already rejected Jesus Christ. The Reverend Billy Graham holds this position. In his book, *The Holy Spirit* he writes:

> All other sins against the Holy Spirit are committed by believers. We can repent of them, be forgiven, and make a new start. Not so with blasphemy of the Spirit. This sin is committed by unbelievers and is often called the unpardonable sin.[2]

In another reference, Dr. Graham broadens the category of those he feels may be guilty of the unpardonable sin.

> There are some so-called theologians today who deny the incarnation—they reject the deity of Christ. In so doing they come very close to blaspheming the Holy Spirit.[3]

But let me share a scriptural analysis that shows blasphemy against the Holy Spirit was committed by men who were initially *believers* in Jesus, men who only later sought to discredit and destroy Him.

John 8 records the series of circumstances in which *believing* Jews later become so offended at some of Jesus' teaching they blaspheme against the Holy Spirit by accusing Him of being demon-possessed. Examining the sequences of events that led to their sin we may come to see how, conceivably, offended believers today might become guilty of committing the same sin.

1. "Even as he [Jesus] spoke, *many put their faith* [Greek *episteusan*] *in him*" (John 8:30, italics added). The phrase "put their faith in him" here means they believed Jesus was the one who was to come, the Messiah. They were like the Samaritans in John 4:42, KJV, who said, "*We believe* [Greek *episteusan*] ... *and know that this is indeed the Christ* [*Messiah*], *the Saviour of the world.*"

Of course, Bible scholars are seldom in complete agreement

---

[2] *The Holy Spirit*, Billy Graham, Word Books, Waco, Texas, 1978, p. 181–182.
[3] Graham, p. 41.

about controversial passages. Some, perhaps reluctant to admit a believer could commit the unpardonable sin, would say that the "faith" of the Jews spoken about in John 8:30 was not really faith. Merrill Tenney in his exposition of the Gospel of John in *The Expositor's Bible Commentary* says of this verse, "The validity of the belief referred to here seems questionable."[4]

But then, in commenting on the next verse, which reads:

> To the Jews *who had believed* (Gr. *pepisteukotas*) *him* Jesus said, "If you hold to my teaching, you are really my disciples. Then you will know the truth, and the truth will set you free."
>
> John 8:31, italics added

Tenney seems to temper his doubt. He says:

> There must have been some sort of avowal of faith by the Jews that evoked the author's comment "to the Jews who had believed him." Jesus evidently began his discourse with the assumption that they, having declared an initial faith, would proceed to a further commitment on the basis of his teaching.[5]

I believe the context clearly supports the argument that the Jews guilty of blaspheming the Holy Spirit were *believers* who became increasingly upset as Jesus probed their legalism.

2. When Jesus spoke to them of their need to be "set free," they took offense and things went quickly from bad to worse. As "sons of Abraham" the Jews claimed they had never been in bondage to anyone and didn't need to be "set free." Later, when Jesus said He knew they were angry enough to kill him . . .

3. "The Jews answered him, 'Aren't we right in saying that you are . . . demon-possessed!' " (verse 48).

---

[4] Merrill C. Tenney, *The Expositor's Bible Commentary*, Regency Reference Library, Zondervan Publishers, Grand Rapids, Mi., Vol. 9, p. 94.
[5] Tenney, p. 95.

4. "Now we know that you are demon-possessed!" (verse 52).

So if Jews "who had believed him" could later become so offended they claimed he was demon-possessed and was "casting out demons by the prince of demons," what about Christians today who become so offended at other believers that they denounce their ministries as Satanic? Even Jesus Himself reminds us that whatever we do to a brother or sister we also do to Him. (See Matthew 25:40.) Could such denunciation today also qualify as blasphemy against the Holy Spirit? Even the thought of committing a sin that might never be forgiven should still the critical tongue of every believer.

Now let us take our projection one step further. If a Christian is guilty of committing a sin that cannot be forgiven, then what is his eternal status? Does he enter into his eternal reward with a black mark against him? Does he become a kind of second-rate citizen of heaven destined to live in his own peculiar section of the Heavenly City? ("See those people over there? They committed the unpardonable sin!")

Or, if a believer is guilty of blasphemy against the Holy Spirit, does he forfeit his salvation? Only God knows.

Nevertheless, there are some statements in Scripture that are quite sobering. For example, 1 John 5:16 speaks of a "sin that leads to death." While John does not specify, he could be referring to blasphemy against the Holy Spirit.

Then, in 2 Peter 2:10–11 there is a lengthy condemnation of false teachers that begins:

> Bold and arrogant, these men are not afraid to slander [blaspheme] celestial beings. . . . [They] blaspheme in matters they do not understand.
>
> 2 Peter 2:10–12

The passage concludes suggesting their judgment will be so severe that they would be better off having never known Jesus as Savior in the first place:

> If they have escaped the corruption of the world by knowing our Lord and Savior Jesus Christ and are again entangled in

it and overcome, they are worse off at the end than they
were at the beginning.

2 Peter 2:20

We do not cite these verses to judge or condemn anyone, only
to note once again that certain sins are more grievous in God's
sight than others, and to voice a sober warning concerning the
danger of blasphemy against the Holy Spirit: That sin endangers
a man's immortal soul.

Why Is Blasphemy Against the Holy Spirit So Terrible?

In chapter thirteen we noted that God does not judge all sin
with equal severity. Some sins seem trivial; others seem deadly.
But since His ways and His thoughts are higher than ours (see
Isaiah 55:8–9), apparently some sins we think are terrible, He dis-
misses with a word, while other sins we consider insignificant, He
judges with great severity.

To the woman taken in adultery, Jesus said, "Neither do I condemn you . . . go now and leave your life of sin" (John 8:11). But
in dealing with the hypocrisy of the Pharisees, He takes the whole
of Matthew, chapter twenty-three, to level seven angry, detailed
indictments against them. Obviously, of the two sins of adultery
and hypocrisy (and adultery is a grievous sin!), God judges hypocrisy more severely. The hypocritical Pharisees condemned the
sinful woman and excused themselves; Jesus forgave the penitent
woman and condemned the Pharisees.

When it comes to blasphemy against the Holy Spirit, we stagger under the weight of Jesus' own words. We dread having to
contemplate thoughts of ultimate rejection, yet the judgment of
God is clearly stated. "But whoever blasphemes against the Holy
Spirit will never be forgiven; he is guilty of an eternal sin" (Mark
3:29).

By God's standards the enormity of the transgression warrants
its classification as the final perversion of truth. To bear deliberate
false witness against God Himself, to boast that the Son of God
serves Satan reveals an arrogant attempt to defile the holy nature
of God. Far more than mere lying, it symbolizes the devil's con-

tinuing but futile effort to capture and corrupt the throne of heaven. It echoes the sound of a cosmic struggle long since won—that terrible and mysterious pre-Adamic event in which God judged a prideful and arrogant Lucifer and cast him out of heaven. (See Isaiah 14:12–15 and Ezekiel 28:11–17.) Blasphemy against the Holy Spirit parades before the eyes of men and angels as a perversion so despicable it arouses the eternal wrath of God.

Is it possible, then, that in our deliberate—or perhaps even our careless—denunciation of one another, we may blaspheme the Holy Spirit and commit the unpardonable sin? Surely, the Lord would not have warned us it could happen unless the danger were very real.

In our attempt to understand we need to consider not how casually *we* regard the practice of criticizing and condemning each other, but how seriously *God* regards the sin and the status of anyone committing it.

Even unwitting and unpremeditated wrongdoing can have tragic consequences. Recently, I read a newspaper account of a family of European immigrants to the United States who gathered mushrooms in the back yard of their new home, cooked them, and ate them. Four members of the family died because the mushrooms were deadly. They ate in ignorance but died anyway.

When Jacob sold Esau his birthright for a bowl of lentil stew, the eternal implications of his act were nowhere in view. Nevertheless, the transaction could not be revoked, nor his lost blessing restored, even though he later sought it with bitter tears. (See Hebrews 12:16–17.) Thus we see from Scripture that some acts—even though not premeditated—precipitate results that are irrevocable.

While one is almost reluctant to pursue the topic further, additional observations seem to be in order. In the past twenty-five years, millions of Christians have been baptized in the Holy Spirit with the accompanying biblical evidence of speaking in unknown tongues. They have received the supernatural gifts of the Holy Spirit promised in Scripture and many have become obedient to the command of Jesus to "preach the Gospel, heal the sick, and cast out demons." Yet sadly, thousands of other Christians regularly denounce speaking in tongues, healing the sick, and casting out demons as the work of the devil. Like the Jews of Jesus' day, are they not attributing to Satan the power of God? While it is not our place to judge, I think we can at least agree on the seriousness of the question! We are considering whether or not a Christian can unwittingly commit an eternal sin.

The grave questions we have raised in this chapter are not intended to bring any believer under condemnation, only to stress how serious a matter it is in God's sight when we slander one another. But if the questions serve to instill a more holy fear and reverent awe of God; if they prompt a humble and fervent determination that we will no longer offend Him and each other by our slanderous utterances; if they inspire a greater desire to honor and respect and encourage one another and a greater reluctance to malign or condemn the life or ministry of any other Christian, then this chapter will have served its purpose.

> Finally, brothers, whatever is true, whatever is noble, whatever is right, whatever is pure, whatever is lovely, whatever is admirable—if anything is excellent or praiseworthy—think about such things. . . . And the God of peace will be with you.
>
> Philippians 4:8–9

14

Winning the Deadliest War of All

In chapter twelve we defined the deadliest war of all as the spiritual slaughter we engage in every time we open our mouths to criticize, malign, accuse, or condemn another believer. Much of the motivation for such slander stems from our willingness to be mouthpieces for the devil, whose very name means "slanderer" or "accuser." But part of it comes from our stubborn refusal to make room for those whose traditions and practices are different from our own.

The Scriptures contain many stories that exemplify that very stubbornness. In fact, in Jesus' day Jews hated Samaritans so much they would detour miles out of the way to keep from traveling through Samaritan towns and villages. And when Jesus began a conversation with the Samaritan woman at Jacob's well, she was astonished and said to Him:

> "You are a Jew and I am a Samaritan woman. How can you ask me for a drink?" (For Jews do not associate with Samaritans.)
>
> John 4:9

A Jewish rabbi in the second century wrote, "He that eats the bread of the Samaritans is like to one that eats the flesh of swine." The same kind of prejudice showed itself among Jesus' own disciples:

> "Teacher," said John, "we saw a man driving out demons in your name and we told him to stop, because he was not one of us."
>
> Mark 9:38

There is one particular story in the Old Testament—a classic tale of prejudice and misunderstanding between opposing factions among the twelve tribes of Israel—that speaks with awesome relevance to our subject. It is the story of a trial endured by two-and-a-half of the twelve tribes of Israel who believed they had a unique destiny in God. Because of their convictions they became the objects of deep suspicion and prejudice. They were condemned and almost murdered by the other nine-and-a-half tribes.

The story begins in Numbers 32. The children of Israel, nearing the end of forty years of wandering, were poised on the bank of the Jordan River ready to enter the Promised Land when Moses was approached with a disturbing request from the Reubenites and Gadites (and later half of Manasseh), whom the New International Version refers to as the "Transjordan tribes." They said to him:

> "The land the Lord subdued before the people of Israel [is] suitable for livestock, and your servants have livestock. If we have found favor in your eyes," they said, "let this land be given to your servants as our possession. Do not make us cross the Jordan."
>
> Numbers 32:4–5

Wearied from his forty-year struggle to lead two-and-a-half million murmuring Israelites safely into the Promised Land on the *other* side of the Jordan, Moses' reaction to their request was totally negative. He had never forgotten the evil report of the ten spies that not only prompted Israel's rebellion but provoked God's wrath and led to forty brutal, punishing years of wandering in the wilderness. He was sure he heard in the request of the Transjordan tribes that same sound of rebellion.

> Moses said to the Gadites and Reubenites, "Shall your countrymen go to war while you sit here? Why do you discourage the Israelites from going over into the land the Lord has given them? This is what your fathers did when I sent them from Kadesh Barnea to look over the land. . . . The Lord's anger was aroused that day and . . . he made them wander in the desert forty years, until the whole generation of those who had done evil in his sight was gone. And here you are, a brood of sinners, standing in the place of your fathers and making the Lord even more angry with Israel."
>
> Numbers 32:6–14

The Transjordan tribes explained to Moses that they were not rebelling, either against God or him. In fact, they volunteered to go with their brothers across the river into battle and help them drive their enemies out of Canaan. They promised: "We will not return to our homes until every Israelite has received his inheritance" (verse 18).

On the basis of their promise, Moses agreed that when the other tribes had claimed their inheritance, the land east of Jordan would be theirs.

> "When the land is subdued before the Lord, you may return and . . . this land will be your possession before the Lord."
>
> Numbers 36:22

In Joshua 4 a few brief verses confirm that the men of the Transjordan tribes kept their word to Moses and went into battle across the Jordan with their brothers.

> The men of Reuben, Gad and the half-tribe of Manasseh crossed over, armed, in front of the Israelites, as Moses had

directed them. About forty thousand armed for battle
crossed over before the Lord to the plains of Jericho for war.

Joshua 4:12–13

But the greatest crisis for the Transjordan tribes still lay
ahead—the rejection they would face once they were identified as
rebels. The story resumes in Joshua 22. The wars had ended and
the other tribes had taken possession of their lands. The Transjordan tribes had kept their word, so Joshua, now the leader of Israel, blessed them and told them to return to their inheritance on
the far side of the Jordan.

But before crossing over, the Transjordan tribes paused and
built an altar, an act that infuriated the other tribes who mistakenly assumed they had erected it to Baal. They were ready to kill
them all!

> When they came to Geliloth near the Jordan in the land of
> Canaan, the Reubenites, the Gadites and the half-tribe of
> Manasseh built an imposing altar there by the Jordan. And
> when the Israelites heard that they had built the altar . . .
> near the Jordan on the Israelite side, the whole assembly of
> Israel gathered at Shiloh to go to war against them.
>
> Joshua 22:10–12

The appalling thing here is the zeal with which the nine-and-
one-half tribes turned against their brothers. Casting aside the
years of loyal support from the Transjordan tribes, they were
ready to commit murder. Words of warning Jesus gave to His disciples centuries later echo their vengeful attitude.

> "In fact, a time is coming when anyone who kills you will
> think he is offering a service to God."
>
> John 16:2

Fortunately, before going to war, a council of leaders from the
other tribes was sent to the Transjordan tribes to lay the charges
of rebellion and idolatry against them.

"How could you break faith with the God of Israel like this?
How could you turn away from the Lord and build yourselves an altar in rebellion against him now?"

Joshua 22:16

The irony is that the council—so certain the Transjordan tribes
were in rebellion because of that altar—was completely mistaken
in its evaluation and totally unjustified in its condemnation.

The Transjordan tribes were shocked to learn that their act had
been so grossly misunderstood. They explained to the council
that the altar was *not* built in rebellion or disobedience, quite the
opposite! They erected it as a sign of their unity with the rest of
Israel. It was to be a reminder for all time that the twelve
tribes—even though some were separated by the river—were one
nation.

"That is why we said, 'Let us get ready and build an altar—
but not for burnt offerings or sacrifices.' On the contrary, it
is to be a witness between us and you and the generations
that follow. . . . Then in the future your descendents will
not be able to say to ours, 'You have no share in the Lord.' "

Joshua 22:26–27

When the members of council learned the real reason the altar
was built, they were stunned to realize how close they came to
murdering innocent men.

"Today we know that the Lord is with us, because you have
not acted unfaithfully toward the Lord in this matter. Now
you have rescued the Israelites from the Lord's hand."

Joshua 22:31

The explanation of the Transjordan tribes as to the real reason
the altar had been erected was all that was needed to resolve the
crisis. Would to God that Christians in sharp disagreement today
could come to such quick and happy solutions to their differences!

Key Factors

It is important that we identify certain key factors in the misunderstanding that arose among the twelve tribes of Israel, since those same factors are present in misunderstandings today. Let us list seven of them.

Nonconformity

The first factor in the misunderstanding between the twelve tribes arose out of the nonconformity of the Transjordan tribes. Nonconformists are always suspect. They never seem content to go along with the crowd! They express strange opinions and have different ideas about how things should be done. Their peculiarities make their friends uncomfortable.

That's the way it was with the Transjordan tribes. Their different vision, their desire to settle on the far side of the Jordan River marked them out as peculiar. And it is a basic characteristic of unregenerate human nature to be suspicious and critical of those who are "different."

Lack of clear communication

How many difficulties in life can be attributed to a failure to communicate! On this occasion, there was obvious fault on both sides. The Transjordan tribes should have told the other tribes they were going to build an altar and why they were building it. After all, they built it before they crossed over to their side of the river.

But that was no excuse for the nine-and-a-half tribes to jump to the wrong conclusion. They were ready to kill their Transjordan brothers, even before choosing the council of ten men. Moreover, that council wasn't sent to discover the truth; it was sent to lay charges of rebellion and idol worship. That's the way too many meetings supposedly called to resolve differences are conducted today; men come together not to discover truth, but to justify their own positions and lay charges against their brothers. So many of the problems among Christians today are the result of poor or inadequate communication!

Hidden suspicion

Suspicion can do more to destroy a relationship than almost any other factor. It is obvious that the suspicions of the nine-and-a-half tribes began years earlier when Moses first accused the Transjordan tribes of rebellion. Unfortunately, Moses' condemnation had such influence that even after his own suspicions were allayed, the power of his words lingered on through the years, sowing deep suspicion and prejudice in the hearts of the other tribes against their Transjordan brothers.

Self-interest

The more people become preoccupied with their own narrow interests, the easier it is to become impatient and critical of others. Self-preservation was an obvious concern of both sides in this controversy. The nine-and-a-half tribes were fearful that the rebellion of their brothers would bring the judgment of God down upon all of them, while the Transjordan tribes were just as fearful of losing their rightful place among the tribes of Israel because they were settling on the far side of the river. Preoccupation with self-interest will always provide ample incentive for misunderstanding and division.

Misinterpreting the evidence

We've all heard the saying "Seeing is believing." Well, there's another—perhaps more accurate—proverb that says, "Don't believe anything you hear and only half of what you see." Painful experience suggests we go slowly in drawing conclusions based on what we see, since what we think we see may not really be the way things are at all. The nine-and-a-half tribes based their condemnation on what seemed to be concrete evidence. Wasn't that altar the Transjordan tribes built indisputable proof they had forsaken Jehovah to worship Baal? The nine-and-a-half tribes were positive their brothers were in rebellion. But to be positive, someone has said,"is to be mistaken at the top of your voice."

The nine-and-a-half tribes were "mistaken at the top of their voices" because they misinterpreted the evidence. Evidence can prove to be a determining factor in any dispute, but only if it is properly interpreted.

The impact of previous problems

More than we are aware, past experiences condition our response to current events. Remember how Moses reacted when he first heard the request of the Transjordan tribes? He said, "You're just like your fathers who brought back an evil report and kept the nation from entering the Promised Land!" His evaluation of their request was impaired by an unpleasant previous experience.

Years ago when I was a pastor in Pennsylvania, a busload of our high school youth attended a rally in Pittsburgh where David Wilkerson was preaching. When several of our young people made personal commitments to the Lord Jesus Christ in that meeting, I was delighted. But one elder and his wife were furious. Only after careful questioning did I discover their reaction stemmed from an unhappy childhood experience of the elder's wife. As a small child she had been terribly frightened by a noisy Pentecostal tent meeting she attended with her parents. Because of that traumatic experience, she had convinced her husband that nothing truly redemptive could come from a "Pentecostal" meeting. In the months that followed they continually referred to the life-changing experiences of our young people as "emotionalism."

Willingness to believe the worst and not the best

It is an unfortunate fact of human nature that we tend to believe the worst and not the best about people. Something sinister and hypocritical lurks just beneath the surface of our religious respectability, which leaves us feeling smug and self-righteous when we hear gossip suggesting that another believer has been found guilty of some gross sin.

How quickly the nine-and-a-half tribes dismissed the years of loyal sacrificial service the Transjordan tribes had given! The very moment they discovered something questionable in the behavior of their brothers, they immediately believed the worst, saying, "Moses was right after all; they are rebels!"

These are some of the common factors that lead to controversy and even persecution among believers. Moreover, they serve as powerful weapons in the devil's hands in the deadliest war of all. Now let's talk about some ways of wresting those weapons from Satan's hands.

Redemptive Steps in Dealing with Controversy and Opposition

> "Why do you look at the speck of sawdust in your brother's eye and pay no attention to the plank in your own eye? How can you say to your brother, 'Brother, let me take the speck out of your eye,' when you yourself fail to see the plank in your own eye?"
>
> Luke 6:41

Human nature does not change; that's why those words of Jesus are as relevant for us today as they were for the people who heard Him speak. If we are ever to win the deadliest war, we must learn constructive ways to deal with our differences. Here are seven specific recommendations, which, if followed, will go a long way toward that end.

Get all the facts and get them straight

Perhaps as much as seventy-five percent of all our misunderstandings with each other stems from our failure to get our facts straight. One of Satan's most successful tactics is to goad Christians into giving exaggerated or biased accounts of the things they have seen or heard. We all know how tales grow in the telling! We don't have to change the story much to create real havoc. For example, in predicting His death and Resurrection Jesus said, "Destroy this temple, and I will raise it again in three days" (John 2:19). But when He was arrested the Jews found witnesses against Him who claimed, "This fellow said, 'I am able to destroy the temple of God and rebuild it in three days' " (Matthew 26:61). The slight alteration of Jesus' statement changed its meaning radically. In His own words Jesus was a man expecting religious martyrdom; but the twisted words of His accusers made Him a violent revolutionary bent on destruction of the temple in Jerusalem.

One small alteration, and truth becomes a lie. Moreoever, even the worst lies of Satan usually contain small portions of truth to make the lie more believable. *Every Christian needs to remember that a half-truth is a lie!*

Don't initiate or repeat gossip and slander

As a minister and Bible teacher who has survived at least three major onslaughts of slander and condemnation in the last thirty years, I can speak from experience about the pain, frustration, and heartache one endures from those who engage in slander. Surprisingly, the attacks usually came, not from unbelievers, but from Christians who professed to love me.

Thirty-five years ago I came to see the scriptural truth about the charismatic gifts of the Holy Spirit. As long as I merely talked about spiritual gifts there was no problem at all. But when I received the baptism in the Holy Spirit with the evidence of speaking in tongues and began to testify to my experience, Christian friends immediately began to accuse me of fanaticism, heresy, mental instability, or being in league with Satan.

Then, eighteen years ago, I was led by the Lord—quite reluctantly—into the ministry of casting out evil spirits. Once more it was Christian friends—mostly charismatics who endorsed other supernatural gifts and ministries of the Holy Spirit—who said I was dividing the body of Christ with dangerous teaching, who said I was demon-possessed and was glorifying Satan in my ministry.

Then twelve years ago, several of us who had been teaching biblical principles of obedience to delegated spiritual authority and the need for commitment and integrity in personal relationships, pledged ourselves to walk together in a covenantal way. Soon, the storm of controversy broke for the third time. All kinds of unsubstantiated accusations were leveled at us. We were accused of trying to take over the charismatic renewal in the church, of usurping control of people's lives, of becoming rich from the tithes of thousands of people (one teacher was reported to be making fifty thousand dollars a week, and another accused of having paid income tax on two million dollars one year!), and of deliberately sowing discord in the body of Christ.

In all three controversies, despite mistakes and imperfect and often inadequate application of the truths God has revealed, time eventually proved the grossest fears and wildest charges of our accusers largely unfounded. Speaking in tongues is not of Satan; those who cast out demons are not demon-possessed; and walking under authority and in the integrity of covenant relationship does not signify financial irresponsibility, bondage, or legalism. Where mistakes and abuses occurred forgiveness has been earnestly sought and usually granted, and significant reconciliation has been achieved.

Fortunately for all of us, it is difficult to sustain hysteria over a long period of time; therefore, most self-appointed spiritual sheriffs have lately found new targets in other parts of the church. Yet even today, a scattered remnant of critics still continue their campaign to discredit these three significant ministries in the body of Christ, as well as the testimony of millions of believers blessed by them. Deliberately ignoring the evidence of myriads of changed lives, these critics continue to cite abuses long since corrected, and continue to carp about failures long since forgiven and forgotten by the majority of Christians who are moving on in faith, rejoicing in the grace of God.

Attribute honest motives to others

The gift of suspicion is not a gift of the Holy Spirit. The quicker we decide to doubt our doubts rather than doubt our Christian brothers and sisters, the better off the whole body of Christ will be. Suspicion is a weapon Satan uses with great skill and effectiveness in his war against the people of God. He tempts us relentlessly to doubt the motives of others and to judge and criticize them for the very same attitudes and acts we justify and give soft names to in ourselves. You're fearful, I'm cautious. You're stingy, I'm careful with money. You're tactless, I'm straightforward. You're a perfectionist, I just like things done correctly. You gossip, I simply speak my mind.

So much pain and division in the body of Christ could be eliminated if we simply decided to follow the golden rule Jesus gave us in the Sermon on the Mount:

> "In everything, do to others what you would have them do
> to you, for this sums up the Law and the Prophets."
> Matthew 7:12

It is so simple to say yet so difficult to do! Without exception, we love to be appreciated; we long for approval. We want everyone to believe our intentions are good, even when our actions fall short. So if we long to have others believe our motives are good and noble, why do we find it so hard to attribute goodness and nobility to their motives?

Is it not jealousy? Why else do we feel secret delight when someone whose success exceeds our own falls on misfortune? Why else the inner anger when someone seeks a privilege we feel should be ours alone? Remember when the mother of James and John asked Jesus if her two sons could be the ones to sit at His right and at His left hand in His Kingdom? Scripture says, "When the ten heard about this, they were indignant with the two brothers" (Matthew 20:24). Why? Obviously because each one of them secretly hoped he would occupy one of the two privileged seats!

It takes a greater longing for unity, and a greater measure of humility than most of us currently hold to give up our suspicions about our Christian brothers and sisters. Still, we must make the effort.

We can begin by making it a point to congratulate friends and associates for their achievements and to express gratitude to God for their contribution to the Kingdom, even as we battle envy and self-pity because recognition and reward came to them rather than us. God knows we cannot control our feelings in such situations, but we can control our words and actions. We can do the right thing, whether we feel good about it or not.

Recognize and allow for legitimate differences

No two snowflakes, no two flowers, no two fingerprints are exactly alike. Since God so obviously delights in variety, why should we expect one Christian to be exactly like another, or one group of believers to share exactly the same traditions or hold exactly the same convictions as another? Beyond the basic convictions we all share concerning the Lordship of Jesus Christ lies an infinite variety of expressions of worship, tradition, and service, each as pleasing to God as the next. The problem lies not so much in our differences as in our own narrow-minded attitude about those differences.

Rather than resenting the blessing of God when it falls on those whose beliefs and practices differ from ours, we should recognize and accept them as a part of the family of God. His blessing shows they are acceptable to Him, therefore they should be acceptable to us as well.

Brother Rufus Moseley, a precious Christian friend whose unique and powerful experiences of the risen Christ tested the credulity of many a conservative believer, told of the reaction of one sincere minister to his testimony. When Rufus had finished speaking, the minister stood up and said, "Brother Moseley reminds me of a visit I once made to an aquarium in a large city. I saw some strange-looking creatures there, the likes of which I never expected to see, but they were fish all right."

Why is it so difficult for us to believe that the Fisher of Men catches many strange-looking fish?

Think of the precious time and energy being wasted by good Christians trying to prove who is right and who is wrong! Every denomination in Christendom today is a testimony not only to loyal adherence to certain significant truths revealed by God, but also to unwillingness to accept additional revelation given to others as well.

I remember painful times in seminary when I would question my theology professor about certain scriptural truths that our denomination ignored or even opposed. "That may be what the Scripture says," he would reply, "but it is not what our denomination believes." To a young minister zealous for the Word of God, such rationalizations were difficult to accept. And after thirty-five years of ministry, I still find them hard to accept.

Allow for human error

Jesus says we are to be perfect, even as our heavenly Father is perfect (Matthew 5:48). The word for "perfect" in the original Greek is the word *teleios*, which is also translated as "mature." The same word is used in Ephesians 4:13:

> [Build up the body of Christ] until we all reach unity in the faith and in the knowledge of the Son of God and become mature [teleios], attaining to the whole measure of the fullness of Christ.

While perfection may never be totally achieved in this life, maturity is an attainable goal. And as long as we remain in these mortal bodies, there will always be room for improvement since at times we not only fail to *do* what is right, we fail even to *want* to do what is right! We're rather like the farmer my father-in-law loved to tell about. A salesman tried to sell the farmer a new tractor he claimed would double his production.

"It's a nice tractor, son," the farmer admitted. "But I don't need it."

"Why not?"

The farmer's logic was unassailable. "Because I'm only farmin' half as good as I know how to now!"

There are times when regardless of faith and conviction, we seem able to farm only half as well as we know how to. At least, that has been my own experience.

When the time comes to give an account for my life, I hope to say I have been faithful and obedient to God at least eighty percent of the time. (On a really good day, I might claim ninety percent; on a bad day, maybe only fifty percent.)

Eighty percent success implies twenty percent failure. What does that twenty percent include? Well, one half, or ten percent, I attribute to ignorance; all those times I have failed—not for lack of effort—but because either I didn't know the right thing to do or I lacked the ability to do it. I've made decisions, preached messages, and given counsel I wish I could recall.

Of the other ten percent, I would say seven percent is due to laziness or lack of initiative. Sometimes I just don't try hard enough. I often display a greater tendency to *let* things happen than to *make* them happen, a trait probably more akin to fault than virtue.

The final three percent, I confess, represents times of stubborn, willful disobedience—clear evidence that I'm not totally redeemed! Like old Jed, sometimes I simply refuse to do the will of God. Jed and Zeke were members of the "spit and whittle club," oldsters who sat around the potbellied stove in the Vermont country store, chewing tobacco, whittling with their pocket knives, and complaining the world was going to the dogs.

One day Jed remarked, "I don't know why the good Lord sees fit to leave me here on earth."

"Perhaps it's because He still has something He wants you to do," volunteered Zeke.

"Maybe so." Jed went right on chewing and whittling. "But I ain't gonna do it!"

That three percent marks those times I find myself deliberately disobedient: doing, saying, or thinking things I know are out of God's will, feeling ashamed and guilty yet seemingly powerless at the moment to make myself stop. Those are the times I know how Paul felt when he said:

> I do not understand what I do. For what I want to do I do
> not do, but what I hate I do. . . . For I have the desire to do
> what is good, but I cannot carry it out.
>
> Romans 7:15, 18

But thank God, He's more interested in the eighty percent than the twenty percent. Since my failure and my sin have already been paid for by Christ's death on the Cross, I have the assurance that when I confess them and ask forgiveness it is immediately granted.

My problem with that twenty percent is twofold. First, I struggle against the devil, who persistently tries to make me feel guilty about my sins even after I know they have been forgiven. Secondly, I struggle with my attitude toward certain other Christians who remember my mistakes long after God has forgotten them, and who seem fully persuaded that the twenty percent reflects the "real me."

I want to say to them, "Don't look at the twenty percent, look at the eighty percent! I don't want to be judged for the stupid, sinful things I've done and said; I want to be remembered for the eighty percent of the time I have managed to be faithful to do and be what God wants. That eighty percent represents the real me, not the twenty percent!" In that desire, I'm sure I'm no different from any other sincere Christian.

Moreover, *I must constantly remind myself that all others who may have hurt or disappointed me are entitled to exactly the same consideration I ask for myself.* I have no more right to point to their twenty percent failure than they have to point to mine, and no more right to ignore their eighty percent success than they have to ignore mine.

Someone has said that tolerance is a forgotten virtue. Nevertheless, if we are to win the deadliest war of all, we must somehow find enough grace to bear with one another's failings and enough maturity to expect no greater measure of perfection in others than we find in ourselves. We must be realistic without becoming pessimistic, remembering that Satan also goads others as well as ourselves into ugly and unchristian behavior, and that the same loving grace that covers our sins, covers theirs as well.

Be quick to forgive

Given the sinfulness of human nature, it is a foregone conclusion that each of us will continue on occasion to err and offend. Therefore, the need for practicing forgiveness can scarcely be overemphasized. Unfortunately, holding grudges is one of those "respectable" sins Christians find so easy to justify and so difficult to forsake.

From my own years of counseling with troubled people, I have learned that most Christians not only gravely underestimate the destructive power of unforgiveness, but they underestimate how much healing and how much redemptive power there is in forgiveness as well. Both those facts point to why God made forgiveness, not an elective course in the curriculum of Christian living, but a required course! We are commanded to forgive!

In fact, forgiving others is such an essential virtue that God deliberately linked it to the grace we seek for ourselves. Thus, every time we withhold forgiveness from others, we endanger our own relationship with the Lord. After teaching that we must forgive others in the same way the heavenly Father forgives us, Jesus adds this warning:

> "For if you forgive men when they sin against you, your heavenly Father will also forgive you. *But if you do not forgive men their sins, your Father will not forgive your sins.*"
> Matthew 6:14–15, italics added

Years ago, I had a sharp professional disagreement with a Christian brother over some matters involving a Christian publication. Since apologies were expressed at the time, I totally forgot the incident until *nine years later* when I received a letter from the man. In the letter he painstakingly recounted every detail of our argument, at first justifying his own position, but finally, almost reluctantly, asking my forgiveness. Obviously, the pain of our encounter was still as sharp for him as the day the argument occurred. I responded quickly, assuring him of my forgiveness and asking his pardon for my own part in the quarrel. But I was also shocked and grieved to realize he had nursed such bitterness for so many years. I found myself praying for him that God would "restore the years the locusts hath eaten" (Joel 2:25, KJV).

Unfortunately, countless numbers of us blunder along day by day nursing similar hurts and grievances, resentments that not only sully our relationship with God and alienate us from those we love, but may radically—perhaps even fatally—affect our health as well.

I remember a prominent clergyman who became bitterly offended at a colleague simply because they disagreed over certain matters of Christian doctrine and practice. When he contracted cancer, some of his closest Christian friends felt his bitterness not only contributed to the onset of the disease but also stood in the way of his recovery. During his illness they repeatedly pled with him to forgive his friend and seek reconciliation. He stubbornly refused and died in his bitterness.

We need also to realize that forgiving others is not dependent on their asking for it. Even though we are the offended party, and even though those who offended us have not sought our forgiveness, we must still forgive. The men who crucified Jesus certainly were not repentant. But even as they watched Him die, Jesus prayed, "Father, forgive them, for they do not know what they are doing" (Luke 23:34).

Once twenty years ago, after I had preached a sermon on the subject, an eighty-year-old widow passed on to me a profound definition of forgiveness she had read somewhere as a child. I have never forgotten it. Neither, I suspect, will you. She said, *"Forgiveness is the fragrance the blossom leaves on the heel of the boot that crushes it."*

One way we can begin to win the deadliest war of all is by refusing to harbor bitterness or resentment against any person, regardless of how we may have been offended or wronged. Many times those who have offended us seem so intractible, the issue so muddled, the grievances so deep, the emotions so overheated, that any human resolution of the conflict seems impossible. In such situations, extending forgiveness may not only be the most *Christlike* thing we can do; it may be the *only* thing we can do. Yet, in the mysterious ways of God, our very act of forgiveness may release the additional grace needed to initiate genuine healing and reconciliation.

Perhaps this may be a good time to mentally review your own relationships and determine if all of them are healthy. As you go down the list, if you find names that seem to make you angry or uncomfortable, or names that remind you of unresolved problems, forgiveness may be in order. Unfortunately, in this day when rights so often seem to take precedence over responsibilities, forgiveness seems a rare and precious commodity. But thank

God we don't have to hoard it. Rather we should squander it, spread it as far and wide as we are able. Life is much too short to spend our days nursing grudges and grievances. Can you imagine what unbelievable healing the whole Body of Christ would experience if all the Christians who are harboring bitterness and resentment against friends, family members, or other believers would obey the Lord and forgive as they have been forgiven?

Take responsibility for what you say

The pain and frustration we bear when being slandered and maligned intensify with the discovery that our accusers seldom seem willing to be accountable for their words. Even when there may be some justification for their criticisms they are still generally unwilling to face us openly, either with evidence or with counsel, which could be the basis of correction and adjustment. Even worse, when the accusations are proven untrue or greatly exaggerated—as such accusations often are—the accusers usually deny accountability for their own sinful gossip saying things like, "Well, that's the way I heard it."

As long as we are the ones making the accusations or spreading the gossip, accountability doesn't seem such a big issue. But when we become the victim of accusation and gossip, then the injustice becomes painfully—and sometimes dramatically—apparent.

As a young Christian of twenty-five, I was attending services at an old historic church in the heart of an eastern city whose godly minister was suffering from a barrage of malicious slander and persecution. One morning as I listened to him preach, he made a brief reference to some of his pain as he spread his arms out wide in a gesture of forgiveness of those who had maligned him. I was stunned to see what appeared to be blood in the palm of each hand. I blinked several times to make sure I wasn't imagining it.

After the service I timidly asked a few people if they had seen anything unusual about the minister's hands during the sermon. One saintly little woman stretched one hand out to me and tapped her palm with her finger. "You saw it too," she whispered.

To this day, I do not know if the stigmata I saw was physically real, or simply a spiritual sign of the very real agony of the minister.

Why do the accusers have such advantage over the accused? And even more ironic is the fact that innocence seldom provides any real solace or protection since most people, including Christians, tend to believe and repeat unsubstantiated accusations.

We mentioned earlier the friend who, after being repeatedly maligned and libeled, finally confronted his accuser only to be laughed at and told he shouldn't take criticism so seriously. Moreover, the man spreading the lies not only failed to offer evidence in support of his accusations, he admitted no wrongdoing and felt no accountability—either to the one he maligned or to anyone else—for his libel and slander.

In chapter nine we listed fifteen recommendations, which, when properly applied, can help prevent a believer from becoming a "false minister." The very first recommendation was that every Christian needs to be submitted to some form of delegated spiritual authority. All of us need to be answerable, to be accountable to some pastor, some elder, some bishop, some superintendent, some Bible teacher—to some person with recognized governmental authority in the church. When we are, we can be held accountable for what we say about each other. We can be required to furnish proof of our accusations or else be required to take responsibility for our slander, apologize, and try to make restitution.

If Christians could be held accountable for what they say, ninety-five percent of the slander and libel running rampant in the church could be eliminated almost overnight, and the "deadliest war of all" could be won in a week.

Unfortunately today, not only the average Christian, but most of the church's leadership, including many men of reputation and authority, fail to act with honor and integrity when speaking about the lives and ministries of others. May God give us the faith and determination to change that presently untenable situation.

An elderly minister friend of mine once told me how he was

conscripted into the Army during World War I. As a young Christian, he was deeply grieved over the war since nations on both sides were considered to be "Christian." While praying, he was given a vision of how terribly God was grieved as well. He was shown how every fatal bullet fired by either side passed first through the body of the Lord Jesus before striking the soldier whose life it claimed.

Could not that vision apply to words as well as bullets? Does not every slanderous word with which we deliberately wound a brother or sister in Christ first wound the heart of Jesus Christ? As He Himself said, "Inasmuch as ye have done it unto one of the least of these my brethren, ye have done it unto me" (Matthew 25:40, KJV).

15

A Call to Commitment

The particular kind of spiritual warfare we have been discussing in the last four chapters, the problem of slander, libel, condemnation, and character assassination waged among God's people, is as old as man himself. Nevertheless, we are responsible for confronting it in our own generation. We have largely failed to do so, not so much from lack of a scriptural mandate, but from lack of resolve and lack of understanding the peril. Until we recognize the war for what it really is—the deadly campaign of an enemy bent on the destruction of the church and the people of God—it seems unlikely that we will ever unite in any significant attempt to win the war.

In our own day large groups of dedicated Christians regularly join together to contend for all kinds of worthy causes: the pro-life movement, church unity, civil rights, nuclear disarmament, you name it. But to my knowledge, there has never been a Christian organization formed or a Christian conference convened to address the problems of slander, libel, and character assassination among believers.

In the previous chapter I listed three major controversies, each with its accompanying onslaught of verbal attack, that I have endured during thirty-five years of ministry: controversy over the baptism in the Holy Spirit and speaking in tongues; controversy over demonology; and the controversy over principles of covenant and spiritual authority, commonly referred to as the "discipleship" controversy.

Yet controversy itself is not the issue. Christians have always differed with one another over matters of church doctrine and practice. When such differences are faced with honesty and integrity, often a greater appreciation of the convictions of others and a clearer understanding of the will of God for everyone has emerged. But the fact that Christians are more apt to berate, condemn, and lie about each other over such differences rather than try to understand each other, is tragic testimony to the devil's continuing success in the deadliest war of all.

Fortunately today, much of the controversy over "discipleship" has subsided as ever-increasing numbers of ministers and churches discover both the scriptural validity and the practical benefits of close pastoral oversight and covenantal integrity among believers, and have begun to apply those principles themselves. As a minister of a large western church said to me recently, "Many of your former critics are now practicing the very disciplines they used to condemn you men for."

Someday, someone will write a definitive work about the discipleship controversy from an unbiased perspective. As one of the original Bible teachers nationally identified with the movement, (the others are Charles Simpson, Bob Mumford, Ern Baxter, and—until 1984—Derek Prince), my perspective is admittedly influenced by personal experience. So with apologies for what may sound like a defense of our position, I want to recount some experiences that illustrate how Satan works to discredit and destroy men and their ministries.

In the early 1970's, as the Holy Spirit began to emphasize to us and to others the biblical principles of pastoral care, covenantal loyalty, and integrity in personal relationships, ministers and churches all across the country began to accept and apply those principles. Some of those ministers and churches had identified with our ministries regularly over a period of years while others had no structural relationship with us at all, happily retaining their denominational affiliation or their independent status.

However, the recovery of any biblical truth always seems to foster controversy. Our own case proved no different. The more the truths we taught were accepted and applied, the more objections and criticisms began to surface. The controversy grew to crisis proportions in 1975 when a nationally prominent minister—who for years had accepted our teaching materials on his radio and television stations—suddenly and publicly denounced our ministries. His action seemed to provoke a veritable barrage of criticism and condemnation against us. His decision was strongly influenced by a particularly malicious report he received condemning one of our small covenant churches in south Florida.

The couple who sent the report had joined the church seeking counsel for a troubled marriage. At first grateful for the help they received, they soon began to chafe under certain spiritual disciplines recommended by the pastor. Eventually they left in anger and circulated their report which was filled with wild accusations against the church, its pastor, and the "Fort Lauderdale teachers." The report accused "discipleship" leaders of assuming total domination over the lives of church members, leaving them incapable of making decisions for themselves, and of stripping them of money and possessions. Moreover, it claimed that in addition to their public services, covenant groups conducted other *secret* meetings where devilish rites reserved only for those in "the inner circle" were practiced. The report further justified its condemnations by noting darkly that Ft. Lauderdale, the home of the "discipleship" teachers, was "the apex of the Bermuda triangle."

One would normally assume that mature Christians—if not rejecting such an account out of hand—would at least hesitate to accept its validity without verification of the wild accusations it contained. Yet no such verification was ever attempted. No questions were asked, no interviews were sought—either with the "Ft. Lauderdale teachers," or the minister, or any other church member—by any responsible person or group of persons to determine if the accusations in the report were valid.

Such behavior on the part of otherwise responsible people clearly indicates how easily Satan stampedes even sincere believers to hasty, ill-conceived conclusions, which may lead to even hastier, ill-conceived actions. Historically, out of such situations, martyrs have been created! Our own investigation indicated that while the young pastor of the church was impatient and sometimes inept in his pastoral oversight, nothing had transpired that could possibly justify the wild accusations of the offended couple. Nevertheless, the report was widely accepted and believed. Similar complaints began to surface across the country as the number of our critics steadily increased.

With the same convenient tunnel vision shown by earlier critics of the baptism in the Holy Spirit and the deliverance ministry, critics of "discipleship" consistently chose to ignore its thousands of grateful adherents and its proven benefits to the body of Christ and concentrated on every reported abuse of authority.

Not surprisingly, many of the criticisms were valid. Historically, every movement seeking to implement the revelation it receives suffers its own mistakes and abuses. Imperfect Christians will faithfully demonstrate their imperfections every time they strive to apply new truth! Moreover, it is a vital part of Satan's strategy to magnify and make public the mistakes of every spiritual pioneer. No one will argue the historic significance of the Protestant Reformation, yet Martin Luther and other Reformers said and did many unwise and unloving things that hindered their holy cause.

Indeed, it is the inevitable fate of reformers to pay not only the price of their own mistakes, and the mistakes of those who imitate them, but also to endure the pain of all kinds of false accusation and vilification. Jesus said:

> "Blessed are you when people insult you, persecute you and falsely say all kinds of evil against you because of me. Rejoice and be glad, because great is your reward in heaven, for in the same way they persecuted the prophets who were before you."
>
> Matthew 5:11–12

Yet it always comes as a shock to discover that those who lay such accusations against us are usually not pagans but staunch believers—often even friends—who have been so quick to suspect our motives and denounce our activities.

Unfortunately, even a genuine offense, before it is dealt with, often fosters condemnation of quite normal activities since the offended party feels obliged to do everything he can to discredit the authority he has rejected. For example, another widely circulated report charged Bob Mumford with saying that he actually claimed to be "God in the flesh." The accuser insisted he had the word of someone who was present in the meeting where Mumford made his boast. His accusation was not only welcomed, but quoted far and wide by many of our critics. Since I was present at the meeting in question, let me explain how what was actually an inspirational event was distorted into an evil accusation.

One night at Bob's large weekly Bible class in Ft. Lauderdale, a young man gave a moving testimony. His marriage had been in deep trouble and through Bob's wise counsel, he and his wife had found fresh hope for their life together. To explain how grateful he was and how pivotal Bob's involvement with them had been, he reminded the congregation of a story Bob had told the previous week, a humorous story about a little boy who became frightened by a thunderstorm and ran and jumped in bed with his parents. They smiled and said, "Don't be afraid, Johnny, God is with you. Go back to your own bed." Reluctantly, Johnny obeyed, only to dive again into his parents' bed with the next flash of lightning and clap of thunder. Before they could speak, he explained, "I know you said God was with me, *but I need someone with skin on!*"

The young man concluded his testimony blinking back tears of gratitude. *"For me and my wife,"* he said, *"Bob Mumford has been 'God with skin on.'"*

That simple, moving testimony was twisted by some offended critic to brand Bob Mumford as a blasphemous egomaniac!

I have some personal recollections of similar accusations. One week during the height of the controversy a young evangelist friend with whom I had once shared several weeks of ministry came for a visit. Parking his car in front of our house, he stared long and hard at our modest home before he entered.

"Have you lived in this house very long?" he asked, as I led him to our small guest room.

"Ever since we arrived in Florida," I replied. "Why?"

"Oh, I was just wondering." He seemed evasive.

The next morning he asked me about the homes of the other teachers. Later that day we drove past the homes of Derek Prince and Bob Mumford, both of whom occupied middle-class homes only moderately more expensive than our own.

"Forgive me for asking, Don," he said as we were returning home, "but how much did you pay for your house?"

"I bought it seven years ago for $28,000," I replied. "It was recently appraised at $44,000."

My young friend took a deep breath and began to share his feelings.

"Don, I owe you and your friends an apology. I've heard some terrible criticisms about your men and your ministries over this 'discipleship' business, and I must confess I believed most of what I heard. According to stories circulating in New England, you men are supposed to have extorted tens of thousands of dollars from your disciples and to have bought luxurious homes for yourselves with the money."

He shook his head and his eyes filled with tears. "But you live in ordinary homes just like everyone else! I ask you to forgive me for believing and repeating some vicious lies about you."

A slightly different accusation was leveled by an angry critic, an influential elder in a church in a small town whose young pastor requested that I provide him with personal spiritual oversight. The young man had been highly successful in his ministry, leading his small church into a period of spectacular growth and spiritual activity, creating considerable jealousy on the part of some other local pastors. The elder, on hearing and believing some vicious gossip about "discipleship," left the church in anger when his pastor refused to renounce his connection with me.

I visited the church four times during the next eighteen months, speaking to his people on weekends and offering pastoral counsel and advice to the young minister. He also contacted me by telephone about once a month. But the angry elder spread the accusation throughout the state that I had "taken over the congregation from its pastor" and that I was "controlling every decision by telephone." The lying elder publicly claimed to have been in the pastor's home and to have seen with his own eyes a telephone bill with long distance charges to my home in Florida in excess of $1000. He claimed the pastor of the church couldn't leave the city limits without getting my permission by telephone.

In still another widely reported abuse of authority an offended believer complained loudly about how his pastor took financial advantage of him.

"While I was out of town, I let my pastor borrow my car," he said. "But when I got the car back I found he had run up a two-hundred dollar repair bill on my car and left me to pay it!" It was the kind of "horror story" our critics love. But investigation by a group of unbiased believers revealed additional facts, which substantially altered the man's story.

The man had owned no car at all until the pastor gave him one of his. The car was given on condition that it be kept in good running order, since the man had a history of abusing his possessions. So when the pastor drove the car and found it in deplorable condition he had the necessary repairs made and left the bill for his grumbling parishioner.

As we have said before, a major factor contributing to misunderstanding is our failure to get all the facts. Remember: *a half-truth is a lie!* The ease and rapidity with which Satan can stir up trouble between us should make our determination to speak about one another with accuracy and integrity a top priority! Perhaps the best way to close this book is by recounting efforts some of us have made to do that very thing.

For over fifteen years, a particular group of Christian leaders has held yearly retreats for the express purpose of developing and maintaining trust and understanding, providing opportunity for men with national ministries to know each other better, and through prayer and fellowship, to overcome the fears and suspicions that so often even cause leaders to criticize and condemn each other. We have come to call the annual retreat the "Charismatic Leaders Conference." Around eighty men are invited each year; usually thirty-five to fifty are able to attend. I have been present at all but one of the retreats.

The first one was held in Seattle, Washington, in 1971. I remember clearly the guarded, suspicious way we looked at each other that first morning. Most of that day was spent in slowly lowering our defenses, and summoning enough courage to speak openly and honestly with one another.

The next three days passed in earnest and sometimes heated discussion about water baptism and demonology. The subject of demons and deliverance was so controversial that at times tempers flared sharply. Ministers who for years had held strong convictions that a Christian could not have a demon or need deliverance, felt that those of us involved in the deliverance ministry were not only in error, but were creating real division in the body of Christ. After one of the sessions, an elderly Pentecostal minister sought me out privately.

"Don, your teaching on the baptism and gifts of the Holy Spirit and your books have blessed many people," he said. "Now you are about to ruin your ministry with this demon business. Everywhere I go, people come to me complaining about your teaching."

I could only remind him how other critics were continually leveling the identical charge at him for promoting the baptism in the Holy Spirit and speaking in tongues. "But you give little weight to their accusations because you know the help your ministry brings to so many," I said. "I feel the same way about the deliverance ministry." Fortunately, the trust and mutual respect that have developed among us through years of meeting together have changed this minister's attitude about deliverance from fierce opposition to loving toleration.

Perhaps the most significant thing to come out of that first retreat was the recognized need for some code of ethics that would outline not only how we should conduct our own ministries, but also how we should speak and act toward each other. The last day of the meeting, a document entitled *Ethics for Christian Leaders* was drafted and solemnly agreed upon, although there was no formal signing of the document. A copy of the document appears at the end of this chapter.

In retrospect I see the verbal acceptance of that code of ethics as a noble, if somewhat ineffective, first attempt to launch a counterattack in the deadliest war of all. I say somewhat ineffective, because within days after our meeting there was renewed verbal attack on some ministers by others who had agreed to abide by the document. When the discipleship controversy flared into the open in 1975, a similar but somewhat larger meeting of leaders reaffirmed that same code of ethics and this time every man present attached his signature to it. But again, the net effect has been less than ideal. Gratefully, we can testify to some progress, but too often the same sincere men who signed the document fall into criticizing, condemning, and maligning each other. The problem is not so much with the code of ethics as with the faltering commitment of some who signed it. Perhaps, to some degree, we have all failed to keep our word.

Yet we must keep on trying.

Surely God is never finished with us. I pray that this book will not only help you who read it to become deeply and prayerfully concerned over the lack of morality and integrity among Christian leaders and laymen alike, but that you will take the noble resolves expressed in the following document and make them your own, and that you will vow to keep them faithfully as God grants grace and strength. I believe nothing would please the heart of God more than for all of us to finally come to that blessed place where we will have repeated our last evil rumor, voiced our last slander, penned our last libelous words, and spoken our last lie against our brothers and sisters in Christ.

> Forgive us our debts as we forgive our debtors. And *lead us not into temptation* but deliver us from evil.
>   Matthew 6:12–13, KJV, italics added

Ethics For Christian Leaders

1. We believe that God has set us in positions of leadership within the body of Christ, either as leaders within a local congregation, or as preachers with a ministry to the body of Christ at large, or in a combination of both these ministries.

2. So far as we are able, we will seek at all times to keep our lives and ministries sound in respect of ethics, morals and doctrine.

3. We will acknowledge and respect all others who have similar ministries and who are willing to make a similar commitment in respect of ethics, morals and doctrine.

4. If at any time we have any criticism or complaint against any of our brother ministers in the body of Christ, we will seek to take the following steps:

First, we will approach our brother directly and privately and seek to establish the true facts.

Second, if thereafter we still find grounds for criticism or complaint, we will seek the counsel and cooperation of at least two other ministers, mutually acceptable to our brothers and ourselves, in order to make any changes needed to rectify the situation.

Finally, if this does not resolve the criticism or complaint, we will seek to bring the whole matter before a larger group of our fellow ministers, or alternatively, before the local congregation to which our brother belongs.

In following these steps, our motive will be to retain the fellowship of our brother and to arrive at a positive, scriptural solution which will maintain the unity of the body of Christ.

Until we have done everything possible to follow the steps outlined in point number four, we will not publicly voice any criticism or complaint against a fellow minister.

In our general conduct toward our fellow ministers and all other believers, we will seek to obey the exhortation of Scripture to "follow after the things which make for peace and things wherewith one may edify another" (Romans 14:19, KJV).